# Instant Chinese

How to Express 1,000 Different Ideas
With Just 100 Key Words and Phrases

by Boyé Lafayette De Mente

## TUTTLE PUBLISHING

Boston • Rutland, Vermont • Tokyo

Published by Tuttle Publishing, an imprint of Periplus Editions
with editorial offices at 153 Milk Street, Boston, MA02109, USA and
130 Joo Seng Road #06-01/03, Singapore 368357

ISBN 0-8048-3374-5

Printed in Canada

Distributed by:

Japan
Tuttle Publishing
Yaekari Building 3F
5-4-12 Osaki, Shinagawa-ku
Tokyo 141-0032, Japan
Tel: (03) 5437 0171
Fax: (03) 5437 0755
Email: tuttle-sales@gol.com

North America, Latin America & Europe
Tuttle Publishing
364 Innovation Drive
North Clarendon, VT 05759-9436, USA
Tel: (802) 773 8930
Fax: (802) 773 6993
Email: info@tuttlepublishing.com
www.tuttlepublishing.com

Asia Pacific
Berkeley Books Pte Ltd
130 Joo Seng Road, 06-01/03
Singapore 368357
Tel: (65) 6280 1330   Fax: (65) 6280 6290
Email: inquiries@periplus.com.sg
www.periplus.com


10 09 08 07 06 05
8 7 6 5 4 3 2

# OTHER BOOKS BY THE AUTHOR

Asian Face Reading: Unlock the Secrets Hidden in the Human
  Face
Business Guide to Japan: Opening Doors...and Closing Deals
Chinese Etiquette & Ethics in Business
Chinese in Plain English
Discovering Cultural Japan: A Guide to Appreciating and
  Experiencing the Real Japan
Etiquette Guide to Japan: Know the Rules...that Make the
  Difference
Instant Japanese: Everything You Need in 100 Key Words
Japanese Business Dictionary: English to Japanese
Japanese Etiquette & Ethics in Business
Japanese Influence on America: The Impact, Challenge and
  Opportunity
Japanese in Plain English
Japan Made Easy—All You Need to Know to Enjoy Japan
Kata: The Key to Understanding and Dealing with the Japanese
Korea's Business and Cultural Code Words
Korean Etiquette & Ethics in Business
Korean in Plain English
Shopper's Guide to Japan
Survival Japanese: How to Communicate Without Fuss or
  Fear—Instantly!
The Chinese Have a Word for It: The Complete Guide to
  Chinese Thought and Culture
The Japanese Have a Word for It: The Complete Guide to
  Japanese Thought and Culture
Japan's Cultural Code Words: 233 Key Terms That Explain the
Attitudes and Behavior of the Japanese
Survival Chinese
Survival Korean (forthcoming)
Instant Korean (forthcoming)
Tokyo Subway Guide: Hundreds of Key Destinations
  (forthcoming)

# Contents

| | | |
|---|---|---|
| 1. | Hello | 9 |
| 2. | Thank You | 9 |
| 3. | Sorry/Excuse Me | 10 |
| 4. | Please | 10 |
| 5. | I | 11 |
| 6. | My/Mine | 13 |
| 7. | You | 13 |
| 8. | Yes/No | 14 |
| 9. | Names | 14 |
| 10. | We | 14 |
| 11. | Speak | 15 |
| 12. | Understand | 15 |
| 13. | Who | 16 |
| 14. | What | 16 |
| 15. | When | 17 |
| 16. | Where | 17 |
| 17. | Why | 18 |
| 18. | How | 18 |
| 19. | This | 19 |
| 20. | That | 19 |
| 21. | Write | 20 |
| 22. | Address | 20 |
| 23. | Introductions | 20 |
| 24. | Family | 21 |
| 25. | Age | 22 |
| 26. | Go | 22 |
| 27. | Come | 23 |
| 28. | Toilet | 23 |
| 29. | Money | 24 |
| 30. | Credit Cards | 25 |
| 31. | Want | 25 |
| 32. | Need | 26 |
| 33. | Airport | 26 |
| 34. | Tip | 28 |
| 35. | Taxis | 28 |
| 36. | Bus | 30 |
| 37. | Subway | 32 |
| 38. | Train | 32 |
| 39. | Walk/Stroll | 34 |
| 40. | Hotel | 35 |
| 41. | Room Service | 37 |
| 42. | Numbers | 37 |
| 43. | Counting Things | 41 |
| 44. | Counting People | 43 |
| 45. | Time | 43 |
| 46. | Days | 47 |
| 47. | Weeks | 49 |
| 48. | Months | 49 |
| 49. | Years | 51 |
| 50. | Drink | 51 |
| 51. | Bar | 52 |
| 52. | Eat | 54 |
| 53. | Dim Sum | 56 |
| 54. | Peking Duck | 56 |
| 55. | Like/Don't Like | 57 |
| 56. | Pay | 57 |
| 57. | Have | 58 |
| 58. | Don't Have | 59 |

| | | |
|---|---|---|
| 59. | Telephone | 59 |
| 60. | Cell Phone | 61 |
| 61. | Computer | 61 |
| 62. | Internet/Email | 62 |
| 63. | Seasons | 63 |
| 64. | Weather | 63 |
| 65. | Meet/Meeting | 64 |
| 66. | Buy | 65 |
| 67. | Shopping | 66 |
| 68. | Gifts | 68 |
| 69. | Cost/Price | 68 |
| 70. | Newsstand | 69 |
| 71. | Post Office | 69 |
| 72. | Sightseeing | 70 |
| 73. | See | 71 |
| 74. | Travel Agent | 71 |
| 75. | Martial Arts | 71 |
| 76. | Beijing Opera | 72 |
| 77. | Emergency | 73 |
| 78. | Ill/Sick | 73 |
| 79. | Medicine | 74 |
| 80. | Doctor | 75 |
| 81. | Dentist | 76 |
| 82. | Hospital | 76 |
| 83. | Ambulance | 77 |
| 84. | Police | 77 |
| 85. | Embassy | 77 |
| 86. | Lost | 78 |
| 87. | Barber Shop | 79 |
| 88. | Beauty Parlor | 79 |
| 89. | Student | 80 |
| 90. | Read | 80 |
| 91. | Mistake | 81 |
| 92. | Rest | 81 |
| 93. | Rent (Car) | 82 |
| 94. | Bicycle | 82 |
| 95. | Street | 83 |
| 96. | Directions | 83 |
| 97. | Books | 83 |
| 98. | Business | 84 |
| 99. | Great Wall of China | 85 |
| 100. | Goodbye | 86 |

### *Additional Vocabulary*

| | |
|---|---|
| China's Provinces | 87 |
| China's Autonomous Regions | 87 |
| Major Cities in China | 88 |
| Famous Places in Beijing | 90 |
| Famous Landmarks Near Beijing | 92 |
| Famous Shopping Districts in Beijing | 92 |
| Famous Places in Shanghai | 92 |
| Important Signs | 94 |
| Other Countries | 97 |
| Terms With Opposite Meanings | 97 |
| Words A to Z | 98 |

# PREFACE

In 1949 the newly established Chinese government issued an edict making Mandarin the national language of the country and mandating that it be taught in all schools. Today, virtually all Chinese speak Mandarin Chinese, known as *putonghua* (puu-toong-whah) or "the common language," as their first or second language.

This book uses English phonetics to represent the syllables making up Mandarin Chinese, making it possible for total newcomers to the language to communicate quickly and easily on a basic level without any previous introduction to the language.

This approach does not take into account the four "tones" that are part of Mandarin. But not all of the words in the language are spoken in tones, and the phonetic versions presented here are close enough to the "correct" pronunciation that the meaning is generally understandable.

With eight major "dialects" in China [some are actually different enough to be called languages!], the Chinese are used to coping with a variety of accents and variations in the tonal quality of speakers. They are especially tolerant of foreigners who make an effort to speak Chinese, and go out of their way to help them.

Here are a number of important introductory terms to get you started, keeping in mind that the phonetics are designed to be pronounced as English:

| | |
|---|---|
| **China** | *Zhongguo* (Johng-gwoh) 中国 |
| **Chinese Language** | *Hanyu* (Hahn-yuu) 汉语 or |
| | *Zhongwen* (Johng-wern)* 中文 |

*Hanyu* is the literary term for the Chinese language; *Zhongwen* is the term generally used in ordinary speech.

| Chinese (person) | *Zhongguoren* (Johng-gwah-wren) 中国人 |
| **Beijinger** | *Beijingren* (Bay-jeeng-wren) 北京人 |
| **Shanghaiese** | *Shanghairen* (Shanghai-wren) 上海人 |
| **Overseas Chinese** | *Hua Qiao* (Hwah Chiaow) 华侨 |
| **Hong Kong** | *Xiang Guang* (She-ahng Gahng) 香港 |
| **Kowloon** | *Jiulong* (Jow-lohng) 九龙 |
| **Macao** | *Aomen* (Ow-mern) 澳门 |

## 1 Hello *Ni hao* (Nee how) 你好

**Hello (to one person)**
*Ni hao* (Nee how) 你好

**Hello (to more than one person)**
*Nimen hao* (Nee-mern how) 你们好

**Good morning (until about 10 a.m.)**
*Ni zao* (Nee zow) 你早

*informal*

**Good morning (very polite form)**
*Zaoshang hao* (Zow-shahng how) 早上好

*normal*

**Good afternoon / Good evening**
*Ni hao* (Nee how) 你好

*xiawu hao afternoon*
*shangwu hao after 10:00*

**Good night**
*Wan an* (Wahn ahn) 晚安

**Goodbye**
*Zai jian* (Dzigh jeean) 再见

## 2 Thank You *Xiexie* (shay-shay) 谢谢

**Thank you**
*Xiexie* (shay-shay) 谢谢

*feichang gǎn xie*

**Thank you very much**
*Feichang xiexie* (Fay-chahng shay-shay) 非常谢谢

*very*

**Thank you for your hospitality**
*Duoxie ni de kuandai* (Dwoh-shay nee der kwahn-die)
多谢你的款待

**No, thanks** *bu xie*
*Xiexie, bu yao* (Shay-shay boo yee-ow) 谢谢，不要

**Don't mention it / You're welcome**
*Bu keqi* (Boo ker-chee) 不客气

9

## 3 Sorry/Excuse Me *baoqian* (bow-chee-an) 抱歉

**I'm sorry, I apologize**
*Duibuqi* (Dway-boo-chee) 对不起

**I'm very sorry**
*Wo hen baoqian* (Woh hern bow-chee-an) 我很抱歉

**Excuse me (to get attention, make way)**
*Lao jia* (Lao jah) 劳驾     *rang yixia*     *jie guang* – easier

**Excuse me... (may I trouble you)**
*Mafan ni...* (Ma-fahn nee...) 麻烦你

**Excuse me... (may I ask a question)**
*Qing wen...* (Cheeng wern...) 请问

## 4 Please *Qing* (Cheeng) 请

**Please hurry!**
*Qing gankuai!* (Cheeng gahn-kwigh) 请赶快     *kuaidian – a little faster*

**Please be careful**
*Qing xiaoxin yidian* (Cheeng she-ow-sheen ee-dee-an) 请小心一点     *(drop the yi)*

**Come in, please**
*Qing jin* (Cheeng jeen) 请进

**Please sit down**
*Qing zuo* (Cheeng zwoh) 请坐

**Can you please help me?**
*Neng bang wo yixia ma?*
(Nerng bahng woh ee-she-ah mah)
能帮我一下吗?

**Please write it down**
*Qing xie xia lai* (Cheeng shay she-ah lie) 请写下来

**Please write it in Roman letters**
*Qing yong Pinyin xie* (Cheeng yohng Peen-een shay)
请用拼音写

**5** | *Wo* (Woh) 我

**I'm an American**
*Wo shi Meiguoren* (Woh shr May-gwoh-wren)
我是美国人

**I'm British/English**
*Wo shi Yinguoren* (Woh shr Yeeng-gwoh-wren)
我是英国人

**I am** _____
*Wo shi* _____ (Woh shr _____) 我是 _____

| | | |
|---|---|---|
| **Australian** | *Aozhouren* (Ah-oh-joe-wren) 澳洲人 |
| **Canadian** | *Jianadaren* (Je-ah-nah-dah-wren) 加拿大人 |
| **French** | *Faguoren* (Fa-gwoh-wren) 法国人 |
| **German** | *Deguowen* (Duh-gwoh-wren) 德国人 |
| **Japanese** | *Ribenwen* (Ree-bern-wren) 日本人 |
| **Spanish** | *Xibanyaren* (She-bahn-yah-wren) 西班牙人 |

**I am from** _____
*Wo shi* _____ *lai-de* (Woh shr _____ lie-duh)
我是 _____ 来的

| | |
|---|---|
| **Australia** | *Aodaliya* (ah-oh-dah-lee-yah) 澳大利亚 |
| **Canada** | *Jianada* (Jah-nah-dah) 加拿大 |
| **Denmark** | *Danmai* (Dahn-my) 丹麦 |
| **England** | *Yingguo* (Eeng-gwoh) 英国 |
| **France** | *Faguo* (Fah-gwoh) 法国 |
| **Germany** | *Deguo* (Der-gwoh) 德国 |
| **Holland** | *Helan* (Her-lahn) 荷兰 |
| **Ireland** | *Airlan* (Ayer-lahn) 爱尔兰 |
| **Italy** | *Yidali* (Ee-dah-lee) 意大利 |
| **Japan** | *Riben* (Ree-bern) 日本 |

| New Zealand | *Niuxilan* (New-she-lahn) 纽西兰 |
| Norway | *Nuowei* (Noh-way) 挪威 |
| Sweden | *Ruidian* (Rway-dee-an) 瑞典 |
| Switzerland | *Ruishi* (Rway-shr) 瑞士 |
| USA | *Meiguo* (May-gwoh) 美国 |

**I'm here on vacation**
*Wo lai dujia* (Woh lie doo-jah) 我来渡假

**I'm in China on holiday**
*Wo lai Zhongguo luxing* (Woh lie Johng-gwoh lwee-sheeng) 我来中国旅行

**I'm traveling on business**
*Wo zuo shengyi luxing* (Woh zwoh sherng lwee-sheeng)
我做生意旅行

**I'm in China on business**
*Wo lai Zhongguo weile zuo shengyi* (Woh lie Johng-gwoh way-ler zwoh sherng-ee) 我来中国为了做生意

**I am traveling alone**
*Wo dandu luxing* (Woh dahn-doo lwee-sheeng)
我单独旅行

**I don't understand (listening)**
*Wo ting bu dong* (Woh teeng boo dohng) 我听不懂

**I've had enough, thank you**
*Wo gou le, xiexie* (Woh go ler, shay-shay) 我够了，谢谢

**I know**
*Wo zhidao* (Woh jr-dow) 我知道

**I don't know**
*Wo bu zhidao* (Woh boo jr-dow) 我不知道

**I'm not sure**
*Wo bu qingchu* (Woh boo cheeng-choo) 我不清楚

I've (already) eaten
*Wo chi le* (Woh chr ler) 我吃了

**6 My** *Wo-de* (Woh-der) 我的

### These are my bags
*Zhe shi wo-de xingli* (Jer shr woh-der sheeng-lee)
这是我的行李

### My address is _____
*Wo-de dizhi shi* _____ (Woh-der dee-jr shr_____)
我的地址是 _____

### That is my book
*Wo-de shu* (Woh-der shoo) 我的书

**7 You** *Ni* (Nee)* 你

### Are you Chinese?
*Ni shi Zhonguoren ma?* (Nee shr Johng-gwoh-wren mah)
你是中国人吗?

### Are you Japanese?
*Ni shi Ribenren ma?* (Nee shr Ree-bern-wren mah)
你是日本人吗?

### Do you live here?
*Ni zhu zai zhe-ge difang ma?* (Nee joo dzigh jay-guh
dee-fahng mah) 你住在这个地方吗?

### Are you married?
*Ni jiehun-le ma?* (Nee jay-hoon-ler mah) 你结婚了吗?

### Do you have children?
*Ni you haizi-le ma?* (Nee you high-dzu-ler mah)
你有孩子了吗?

*The "you" (*ni*) is generally left out of sentences when it is
understood from the context.

*DUI = CORRECT*

## 8 Yes / No* *Shi* (shr) 是 / *Bu* (Boo) 不

*Yes and no are not commonly used on their own in Chinese.
Yes is usually expressed by repeating the verb. The negative
is expressed by putting *bu (boo)* or *mei (may)* in front of
verbs and adjectives.

## 9 Names *Mingzi* (Meeng-dzu) 名字

**first name** *ming* (meeng) 名    *Wo ming* ——
**family name** *xing* (sheeng) 姓

**What is your first name?**
*Nin gui ming?* (Neen gway-meeng) 你贵名?

**What is your family name?**
*Ni xing shenme?* (Nee sheeng shern-mo) 你姓什么?

**My family name is _____**
*Wo xing _____* (Woh sheeng _____) 我姓 _____

## 10 We *Wo-men* (Woh-mern) 我们

**Where are we? / Where is this?**
*Zhe shi nali?* (Jer shr nah-lee?) 这是那里?

**We are not going**
*Wo-men bu qu* (Woh-mern boo chwee) 我们不去

**We have one daughter**
*Wo-men you yi-ge nuer* (Woh-mern you ee-guh nwee-urr) 我们有一个女儿

**We live in America**
*Wo-men zhu Meiguo* (Woh-mern joo May-gwoh)
我们住美国

**We are married**
*Wo-men jiehun-le* (Woh-mern jeh-hoon-ler) 我们结婚了

14

**We want to go to_____**
*Wo-men yao qu _____* (Woh-mern yee-ow chwee _____)
我们要去 _____

## 11 Speak *Shuo* (Shwo)

**Do you speak English?**
*Ni hui shuo Yingwen ma?* (Nee hway shwo Eeng-wern mah?) 你会说英文吗?

**I don't speak Chinese**
*Wo bu hui Zhongwen* (Woh boo hway Johng-wern)
我不会中文

**I speak a little Chinese**
*Hui yidian Zhongwen* (Hway ee-dee-an Johng-wern)
会一点中文

**Please speak more slowly?**
*Qing shuo man yidian?* (Cheeng shwo mahn ee-dee-an)
请说慢一点?

**What did you say?**
*Ni shuo shenme?* (Nee shwo shern-mo) 你说什么?

**Please repeat that?**
*Qing ni zai shuo yibian?* (Cheeng nee dzie shwo ee bee-an?) 请你再说一遍?

**What did he say?**
*Ta shuo shenme?* (Tah shwo shern-mo) 他说什么?

## 12 Understand *Dong* (Dohng) 懂

**I understand**
*Wo dong* (Woh dohng) 我懂

**I don't understand**
*Wo bu dong* (Woh boo dohng) 我不懂

**We don't understand**
*Wo-men bu dong* (Woh-mern boo dohng) 我们不懂

**Do you understand?**
*Ni dong ma?* (Nee dohng mah) 你懂吗?

**Did you understand?**
*Ni ming bai-le ma?* (Nee meeng by-ler mah) 你明白了吗?

**I need an interpreter**
*Wo xu yao fanyi yuan* (Woh she-yow fahn-ee ywahn)
我需要翻译员

### 13 Who? (question) *Shui* (Shway) 谁?

**Who are you?**
*Ni shi shui?* (Nee shr shway) 你是谁?

**Who is that?**
*Na shi shui?* (Nah shr shway) 那是谁?

**Who is first?**
*Shui shi-de yige?* (Shway shr-dee ee-guh) 谁是第一个?

**Who speaks English**
*Shui neng shuo Yingwen?* (Shway nerng shwo Eeng-wern) 谁能说英文?

### 14 What? *Shenme?* (Shern-mo) 什么?

**What is this called in Chinese?**
*Zheige Zhongwen jiao shenme?* (Jay-guh Johng-wern jow shern-mo) 这个中文叫什么?

**What is that called?**
*Na ge jiao shenme?* (Nah guh jee-ow shern-mo)
那个叫什么?

**What time is breakfast?**
*Jidian chi zaofan?* (Jee-dee-an chr zow-fahn) 几点吃早饭?

**What time is lunch?**
*Jidian chi wufan?* (Jee-dee-an chr woo-fahn)
几点吃午饭?

**What is your address?**
*Ni-de dizhi?* (Nee-der dee-jr) 你的地址?

**What is this street?**
*Zhe shi na tiao jie?* (Jur shr nay-tee-ow jeh) 这是那条街?

**What is that?**
*Na shi shenme?* (Nah shr shern-mo) 那是什么?

## 15 When? *Shenme shihou?* (Shern-mo shr-hoe) 什么时候?

**When are we going?**
*Wo men shenme shihou qu?* (Woh-mern shern-mo shr-hoe chwee) 我们什么时候去?

**When will you be finished?**
*Ni shenme shihou hui hao?* (Nee shern-mo shr-hoe hway how) 你什么时候会好?

**When does it begin?**
*Shenme shihou kaishi?* (Shern-mo shr-hoe kigh-shr?) 什么时候开始?

## 16 Where? *Nali?* (Nah-lee) 那里?/ *Nar?* (Nah-urr) 那儿?

**Where is ____?**
____ *zai na?* (____ zigh nah-urr) ____ 在那?

**Where is it?**
*Ta zai nali?* (Tah zigh nah-lee) 它在那里?

**Where are you from?**
*Ni shi cong na lai-de?* (Nee shr tsohng nah-urr lie-der)
你是从那来的?

**Where do you want to go?**
*Ni xiang qu nali?* (Nee she-ahng chwee nah-lee)
你想去那里？

**Where are we going?**
*Wo men yao qu nali?* (Woh-mern yow chwee nah-lee)
我们要去那里？

ZAI NAR?

**Where is my friend?**
*Wo de pengyou zai nali?* (Woh-der perng-you zigh nah-lee) 我的朋友在那里？

**Where is the bus stop?**
*Che zhan zai nali?* (Cher jahn zigh nah-lee) 车站在那里？

**17 Why?** *Weishenme?* (Way shern-mo) 为什么？

**Why? (whenever needed)**
*Weishenme?* (Way-shern-mo) 为什么？

**18 How?** *Duo?* (Dwoh) 多; *Zenme?* (Zern-mo) 怎么？

**How much is it/that?**
*Duo shao qian?* (Dwoh shou chee-an) 多少钱？

**How much is this?**
*Zhe shi duo shao?* (Jur shr dwoh-shou) 这是多少？

**How does this work?**
*Zhe zenme caozuo?* (Jur zern-mo chow zwoh)
这怎么操作？

**How far is it?**
*Li zhe duo yuan?* (Lee juh dwoh ywahn) 离这多远？

**How long will it take?**
*Zhe yao duo jiu?* (Juh yow dwoh jeo) 这要多久？

## 19 This *Zhe* (Jur) 这; *Zhei* (Jay) 这

**This is mine**
*Zhe shi wo-de* (Jur shr woh-der) 这是我的

**What is this?**
*Zhe shi shenme?* (Juh shr shern-mo) 这是什么?

**I don't like this (it)**
*Bu xihuan* (Boo she-hwahn) 不喜欢

**How much is this?**
*Zhe shi duoshao?* (Jur shr dwoh-shou) 这是多少?

**This is very good**
*Zhe hen hao* (Jur hern how) 这很好

## 20 That *Na* (Nah) 那 / *Nei* (Nay) 那

**What is that?**
*Na shi shenme?* (Nah shr shern-mo) 那是什么?

**That's my luggage**
*Na shi wo-de xingli* (Nah shr woh-der sheeng-lee)
那是我的行李

**Is that so?**
*Shi ma?* (Shr mah) 是吗?

**How much is that?**
*Na shi duoshao?* (Nah shr dwoh-shou) 那是多少?

**Who is/was that?**
*Na shi shei?* (Nah shr shay) 那是谁?

**What is that street?**
*Na shi neitiao jie?* (Nah shr nay-tee-ow jeh)
那是那条街?

19

**21 Write** *Xie* (Shay) 写

**Please write it down**
*Qing ni xie xia* (Cheeng nee shay shah) 请你写下

**Please write it in Roman letters**
*Qing yong pinyin xie* (Cheeng yohng peen-yeen shay) 请用拼音写

**Please write it in Chinese**
*Qing yong Zhongwen xie* (Cheeng yohng Johng-wern shay) 请用中文写

**22 Address** *Dizhi* (dee-juh) 地址

**(This is) my address**
*Wo-de dizhi* (Woh-der dee-jr) 我的地址

**What is your address?**
*Ni-de zhu zhi shi?* (Nee-der joo jr shr) 你的住址是？

**Please write it down**
*Qing xie xia lai* (Cheeng shay shah lie) 请写下来

**Please read it to me**
*Qing du zhe-ge gaiwo ting* (Cheeng doo jur-guh guy-woh ting) 请读这个给我听

**Please read it out loud**
*Qing da sheng du* (Cheeng dah sherng doo) 请大声读

**23 Introductions** *Jieshao* (Jeh-shou) 介绍

**May I introduce myself?**
*Wo keyi jieshao woziji ma?* (Woh ker-ee jeh-shou woh-dzu-jee mah) 我可以介绍我自己吗？

**My name is _____**
*Wo-de mingzi shi _____* (Woh-der meeng-dzu shr _____)
我的名字是 _____

**This is my name card**
*Zhe shi wo-de ming pian* (Jur shr woh-der meeng pee-an)
这是我的名片

**What is your name?**
*Ni jiao shenme mingzi?* 你叫什么名字?
(Nee jow shern-mo meeng-dzu)

**I'm pleased to meet you**
*Jiuyang* (Joe-yahng) 久仰

**Do you have a name card?**
*Ni you ming pian ma?* (Nee you meeng pee-an mah)
你有名片吗?

**This is my wife**
*Zhe shi wo-de furen* (Jur shr woh-der foo-wren)
这是我的夫人

### 24 Family *Jiawren* (jah-wren) 家人

| | |
|---|---|
| **husband** | *zhangfu* (jahng-foo) 丈夫 |
| **wife** | *furen* (foo-wren) 夫人 |
| | *qizi* (chee-dzu) 妻子 |
| **children** | *haizi* (high-dzu) 孩子 |
| **daughter** | *nuer* (nwee-urr) 女儿 |
| **son** | *erzi* (urr-dzu) 儿子 |

**Do you have children?**
*You haizi ma?* (You high-dzu mah) 有孩子吗?

**I have two daughters**
*You liang-ge nuer* (You lee-ahng-guh nwee-urr)
有两个女儿

**Are you married?**
*Jiehunle ma?* (Jeh hoon-ler mah) 结婚了吗?

**I'm married**
Jiehunle (Jeh hoon-ler) 结婚了

**I'm single**
Mei jiehun (May jeh-hoon) 没结婚

**This is my wife**
Zhewei shi wo qizi (Jur-way shr woh chee-dzu)
这位是我妻子

**This is my husband**
Zhewei shi wo zhangfu (Jur-way shr woh jahng-foo)
这位是我丈夫

**25 Age** Nianling (Nee-an-leeng) 年龄; Sui (Sway) 岁

**How old are you (to young children)**
Ni ji sui? (Nee jee sway) 你几岁?

**How old are you (to all others)**
Ni duo da? (Nee dwoh dah) 你多大?

**26 Go** Qu (Chwee) 去

**I am going**
Qu (Chwee) 去 *(I) Go.*

**I'm not going**
Bu qu (Boo chwee) 不去 *(I) NO Go.*

**Are you going?**
Ni qu ma? (Nee chwee mah) 你去吗?

**Is he/she going**
Ta qu ma? (Tah chwee mah) 他去吗?

**Are they going?**
Ta-men qu ma? (Tah-mern chwee mah) 他们去吗?

**Are we going now?**
*Wo-men xianzai qu ma?* (Woh-mern shee-an-zigh chwee mah) 我们现在去吗?

## 27 Come *Lai* (Lie) 来

**I'm coming**
*Wo lai* (Woh lie) 我来

*I Come.*

**I'm not coming**
*Wo bu lai* (Woh boo lie) 我不来

**He/she is coming**
*Ta lai* (Tah lie) 他来

**He/she is not coming**
*Ta bu lai* (Tah boo lie) 他不来

*NENG — CAN*

**I cannot come**
*Bu neng lai* (Boo nerng lie) 不能来

*NO CAN Come.*

**They are coming**
*Ta-men lai* (Tah-mern lie) 他们来

**I will come tomorrow**
*Wo mingtian lai* (Woh meeng-tee-an lie) 我明天来

## 28 Toilet *Cesuo* (tser-swoh) 厕所

| men | *nan* (nahn) 男 |
| women | *nu* (nwee) 女 |
| public toilet | *gonggong cesuo* (gohng-gohng tser-swoh) 公共厕所 |

**Where is the toilet, please?**
*Qingwen, cesuo zai nar?* (Cheeng-wern, tser-swoh dzigh nah-urr) 请问，厕所在那儿?

**Is there a public toilet near here?**
*Zhe fujin you gonggong cesuo ma?* (Jur foo-jeen you gohng-gohng tser-swoh mah) 这附近有公共厕所吗?

**I need to go to the toilet**
*Wo yao qu cesuo* (Woh yee-ow chwee tser-swoh)
我要去厕所

## 29 Money *Qian* (Chee-an) 钱

| | | |
|---|---|---|
| Chinese currency | *KWAI* *renminbi* (wren-meen-bee) 人民币 YUAN | |
| US dollars | *Mei yuan* (May ywahn) 美元 | |
| Hong Kong dollars | *Gang bi* (Gahng bee) 港币 | |
| Australian dollars | *Aodaliya yuan* (Ah-aw-dah-lee-yah ywen) 奥地利亚元 | |
| Canadian dollars | *Jiabi* (Jee-ah-bee) 加币 | |
| English pounds | *Ying bang* (Yeeng bahng) 英镑 | |
| Japanese yen | *Ri yuan* (Ree ywahn) 日元 | |
| travelers' checks | *luxing zhipiao* (lwee-sheeng jr-pee-ow) 旅行支票 | |
| credit cards | *xinyong ka* (sheen-yohng kah) 信用卡 | |
| cash | *xiankuan* (shee-an-kwahn) 现款 | |

**Where can I exchange money?**
*Nali keyi duihuan qian?* (Nah-lee ker-ee dway-hwahn chee-an) 那里可以兑换钱?

**What is today's exchange rate for US dollars?**
*Jintian Mei yuan duihuan lu duoshao?* (Jeen-tee-an May ywahn dway-hwahn lwee dwoh-shou)
今天美元兑换率多少?

**Can you write it down?**
*Ni neng xiexia-lai ma?* (Nee nung shay-she-ah lie mah)
你能写下来吗?

## 30 Credit Cards *Xinyong ka* (Sheen-yohng kah)
信用卡

### Do you accept credit cards?
*Ni shou xinyong ka ma?* (Nee show sheen-yohng kah mah) 你收信用卡吗?

### Which credit cards do you accept?
*Ni-men jieshou naxie xinyong ka?* (Nee-mern jeh-show nah-shay sheen-yohng kah) 你们接受那些信用卡?

### Can I use my credit card to get cash?
*Wo neng yong xinyong ka duihuan xiankuan ma?* (Woh nerng yohng sheen-yohng kah dway-hwahn shee-an-kwahn ma) 我能用信用卡兑换现款吗?

## 31 Want *Yao* (yow) 要

### I want to go to the Great Wall
*Wo yao qu Chang Cheng* (Woh yow chwee Chahng Cherng) 我要去长城

### I want to go sightseeing
*Wo yao qu guanguang* (Woh yow chwee gwahn-gwahng) 我要去观光

### I want to buy a newspaper
*Wo yao mai baozhi* (Woh yow my bow-jr) 我要买报纸

### I want to go to the American Embassy
*Wa yao qu Meiguo Dashiguan* (Woh yow chwee May-gwoh Dah-shr-gwahn) 我要去美国大使馆

### I want to rest
*Wo yao xiuxi* (Woh yee-ow she-oh-she) 我要休息

ALREADY = yǐ jīng

## 32 Need *Xuyao* (She-yee-ow) 需要

### I need some aspirin
*Wo xuyao asipilin* (Woh she-yee-ow ahs-pee-leen) 我需要阿司匹林

*Wǒ xuyào*

### I need some foot powder
*Wo xuyao jiao zhi fen* (Woh she-yee-ow jee-ow chee fern) 我需要脚指粉

### I need some shampoo
*Wo xuyao xifaji* (Woh she-yee-ow see-fa-jee) 我需要洗发剂

### I need some razor blades
*Wo xuyao guahu dao* (Woh she-yee-ow gwah-hoo dow) 我需要刮胡刀

### I need some eyedrops
*Wo xuyao yanyao shui* (Woh she-yee-ow yahn-yee-ow shway) 我需要眼药水

### I need an umbrella
*Wo xuyao yusan* (Woh she-yee-ow yuh-sahn) 我需要雨伞

## 33 Airport *Feijichang* (Fay-jee-chahng) 飞机场

| | |
|---|---|
| airport shuttle bus | *jichang jie songche* (jee-chahng jee-eh sohng-cher) 机场接送车 |
| airplane | *feiji* (fay-jee) 飞机 |
| airline | *hangkong gongsi* (hahng-kohng-gohng-suh) 航空公司 |
| hotel shuttle bus | *luguan jie songche* (lwee-gwahn jee-eh sohng-cher) 旅馆接送车 |
| flight number | *hangban haoma* (hahng-bahn how-mah) 航班号码 |
| reservations | *yuding* (yuu-deeng) 预定 |

26

*Nǐ hěn tè bié!*
*You (Are) Very special!*

| | |
|---|---|
| ticket | *piao* (pee-ow) 票 |
| first-class | *toudeng-cang* (toe-derng tsahng) 头等舱 |
| first-class ticket | *toudeng piao* (toe-derng pee-ow) 头等票 |
| economy class | *jingji cang* (jeeng-jee tsahng) 经济舱 |
| economy class ticket | *putong piao* (poo-tohng pee-ow) 普通票 |
| confirm | *queren* (chwee-uh-wren) 确认 |
| connecting flight | *xianjie hangban* (shee-an jee-eh hahng-bahn) 线接舱班 |
| boarding card | *dengji ka* (derng-jee kah) 登机卡 |
| carry-on baggage | *shouti bao* (show-tee bow) 手提包 |
| aisle seat | *kaozou dao zuowei* (kow-zow dow zwoh-way) 靠走道坐位 |
| window seat | *kaochuang zuowei* (kow-chwahng zwoh-way) 靠窗座位 |
| passport | *huzhao* (hoo-jow) 护照 |

### Please help me with my luggage

*Qing ni bang wo ban xingli* (Cheeng nee bahng woh bahn sheeng-lee) 请你帮我搬行李

### Where do I wait for the hotel shuttle bus?

*Zai nali deng luguan de bashi?* (Dzigh nah-lee derng lwee-gwahn der ba-shr) 在那里等旅馆的巴士？

### Is this the line for the shuttle bus?

*Zai zheli paidui deng luguan bashi ma?* (Dzigh jur-lee pah-dway lwee-gwahn ba-shr mah) 在这里排队等旅馆巴士吗？

### Where can I get a taxi?

*Nali you chuzu qiche?* (Nah-lee you choo-joo chee-cher) 那里有出租汽车？

THIS IS VERY SPECIAL!
ZHÈ SHÌ HĚN TÈ BIÉ!

TÈ BIÉ
(TÖ Beeyeh

### 34  Tip *Xiaofei* (Shou-fay) 小费

**Is tipping permitted here?**
*Zhe-li keyi gei xiaofei ma?* (Jur-lee ker-ee gay shou-fay mah? 这里可以给小费吗?

**How much should I tip?**
*Yinggai gei duoshao xiaofei?* (Yeeng-guy gay dwoh-shou shou-fay) 应该给多少小费?

**This tip is for you**
*Zhe xiaofei shi gei ni-de* (Jur shou-fay shr gay nee-der) 这小费是给你的

### 35  Taxi *Chuzuqiche* (Choo-joo-chee-cher) 出租汽车

| taxi stand | *chuzuqiche zhan* (choo joo chee-cher jahn) 出租汽车站 |
| fare | *piaojia* (pee-ow-jah) 票价 |

**Where can I get a taxi?**
*Chuzu qiche zai nar?* (Choo-joo chee-cher dzigh nah-urr) 出租汽车在那儿?

**Is there a taxi stand near here**
*Zhe fujin you chuzu qiche zhan ma?* (Jur foo-jeen yow choo-joo chee-cher jahn mah) 这附近有出租汽车站吗?

**Please call a taxi for me**
*Qing gei wo jiao che* (Cheen gay woh jow cher) 请给我叫车

**I want to go to ____**
*Wo yao qu ____* (Woh yow chwee ____) 我要去 ____

**Please take me to ____**
*Qing song wo dao ____* (Cheeng sohng woh dow ____) 请送我到 ____

TAKE = SONG
      = DAI ✓

### Please take me to the airport
*Qing dai wo dao feiji chang* (Cheeng die woh dow fay-jee chahng) 请带我到飞机场

### The airport, please
*Qing qu jichang* (Cheeng chwee jee-chahng) 请去机场

### I'm in a hurry
*Wo gan shijian* (Woh gahn shr-jee-ann) 我赶时间

### How long will it take to get to the airport?
*Dao jichang yao duoshao shijian?* (Dow jee-chahng yow dwoh-shou shr-jee-an?) 到机场要多少时间?

### Please take me to my hotel
*Qing dai wo dao wo-de luguan* (Cheeng die woh dow woh-der lwee-gwahn) 请带我到我的旅馆

### Please pick me up at _____
*Qing dao _____ jie wo* (Cheeng dow _____ jee-eh woh) 请到 _____ 接我

### Please come back at _____
*Qing ____ hui lai* (Cheeng ____ hwee lie) 请 ____ 回来

### Please take me to this address
*Qing dai wo dao zhe-ge dizhi* (Cheeng die woh dow jay-guh dee-jr) 请带我到这个地址

### Please go to Tiananmen Square
*Qing qu Tiananmen Guang Chang* (Cheeng chwee Tee-an-ahn-mern Gwahng Chahng) 请去天安门广场

### Can you wait for me?
*Ni neng deng wo ma?* (Nee nerng derng woh mah) 你能等我吗?

NENG = CAN
DENG = WAIT

### Please wait for me
*Qing ni deng yi deng* (Cheeng nee derng ee derng) 请你等一等

zhù nǐ kāi xīn!   HAVE A GOOD DAY!

29

**How much do I owe you?**
*Gai fu duoshao qian?* (Guy foo dwoh-shou chee-an)
该付多少钱?

**How much?**
*Duo shao qian?* (Dwoh shou chee-an) 多少钱?

## 36 Bus *Qiche* (Chee-cher) 汽车

| | |
|---|---|
| **central bus station** | *qiche zhong zhan* (chee-cher zohng jahn) 汽车终站 |
| **bus station** | *gonggongqiche zhan* (gohng-gohng-chee-cher jahn) 公共汽车站 |
| **bus stop** | *qiche zhan* (chee-cher jahn) 汽车站 |

**Is there a bus stop near here?**
*Zhe fujin you qiche zhan ma?* (Jr foo-jeen yow chee-cher jahn mah) 这附近有汽车站吗?

**Where is the bus station?**
*Gonggong qiche zhanzai nali?* (Gohng-gohng chee-cher jahn dzigh nah-lee) 公共汽车站在那里?

**How do I get to the bus station?**
*Dao qiche zhan zenme zou?* (Dow chee-cher jahn zern-mah dzow) 到汽车站怎么走?

**Which bus do I take to get to Tiananmen Square?**
*Dao Tiananmen zuo ji lu che?* (Dow Tee-an-ahn-mern zwoh jee loo cher) 到天安门坐几路车?

**Is it necessary to change buses?**
*Yao huan che ma?* (Yow hwahn cher mah) 要换车吗?

**How much is the fare?**
*Piaojia duoshao?* (Pee-ow jah dwoh-shou) 票价多少?

### Do you have a map of the city?

*Nimen you meiyou shi ditu?* (Nee-mern you may-you shr dee-too) 你们有没有市地图？

### Do you have a brochure about the city?

*Nimen you meiyou ben shi jieshao shu?*
(Nee-mern you may-you bern jee-eh-shaow shoo)
你们有没有本市介绍书？

### Do you have a bus timetable, please?

*Qing gei wo yige gonggong qiche shikebiao?*
(Cheeng gay woh ee-guh gohng-gohng chee-cher shr-ker beow) 请给我一个公共汽车时刻表。

### Please take me to the bus station

*Qing dai wo dao gonggong qi chezhan*
(Cheeng die woh dow gohng-gohng chee cher-jahn)
请带我到公共汽车站

### Where does the bus for downtown leave from?

*Qu chengli de gonggong qiche cong nar kai?*
(Chwee cherng-lee der gohng-gohng chee-cher tsohng narr kigh) 去城里的公共汽车从那儿开？

### Where does the bus for the airport leave from?

*Qu feijichang de gonggong qiche cong nar kai?*
(Chwee fay-jee-chahng der gohng-gohng chee-cher tsohng narr kigh) 去飞机场的公共汽车从那儿开？

### Is this the bus for the aiport?

*Zhe shi bu shi qu jichang de gonggong qiche?*
(Jay shr boo shr chwee jee-chahng der gohng-gohng chee-cher) 这是不是去机场的公共汽车？

### How much is it to the airport?

*Feijichang duoshao qian?* (Fay-jee-chahng dwoh-shou chee-an) 飞机场多少钱？

**What time is the bus leaving?**
*Gonggong qiche jidian likai?* (Gohng-gohng chee-cher jee-dee-an lee-kigh) 公共汽车几点离开?

## 37 Subway *Ditie* (Dee-tee-eh) 地铁

**subway station**   *ditie zhan* (dee-tee-eh jahn) 地铁站

**Where is the nearest subway station?**
*Zuijin de dixiatie che zhan zai nali?* (Zway-jeen der dee-shah-tee-eh cher jahn zigh nah-lee)
最近的地下铁车站在那里?

**Let's go by subway**
*Wo men zuo dixiatie qu* (Woh-mern zwoh dee-shah-tee-eh chwee) 我们坐地下铁去

## 38 Train *Huoche* (Hwoh-cher) 火车

| | |
|---|---|
| **China National Railways** | *Zhongguo Tielu* (Johng-gwoh Tee-eh-loo) 中国铁路 |
| **train station** | *huoche zhan* (hwoh-cher jahn) 火车站 |
| **local (ordinary) train** | *putong che* (poo-tohng cher) 普通车 |
| **express train** | *kuai che* (kwie cher) 快车 |
| **slow train** | *man che* (mahn cher) 慢车 |
| **ticket** | *piao* (pee-ow) 票 |
| **train ticket** | *che piao* (cher-pee-ow) 车票 |
| **ticket office** | *shou piao chu* (show pee-ow choo) 售票处 |
| **one-way ticket** | *dan cheng piao* (dahn cherng pee-ow) 单程票 |
| **round-trip ticket** | *laihui piao* (lie-hway pee-ow) 来回票 |

| | |
|---|---|
| **first-class ticket** | *tou-deng piao* (toe-derng pee-ow) 头等票 |
| **economy-class ticket** | *putong piao* (poo-tohng pee-ow) 普通票 |
| **soft-class (ticket)** | *ruan zuo* (rwahn zwoh) 软座 |
| **hard-class (ticket)** | *ying zuo* (eeng zwoh) 硬座 |
| **soft sleeper** | *ruan wo pu* (rwahn woh poo) 软卧铺 |
| **hard sleeper** | *ying wo pu* (eeng woh poo) 硬卧铺 |
| **compartment** | *chexiang* (cher-she-ahng) 车厢 |
| **reserved seat ticket** | *yuding zuowei piao* (yuu-deeng zwoh-way pee-ow) 预定座位票 |
| **unreserved seat ticket** | *wu yuding zuowei piao* (woo yuu-deeng zwoh-way pee-ow) 无预定座位票 |
| **fare** | *chefei* (cher-fay) 车费 |
| **boarding platform** | *yuetai* (yuu-eh-tie) 月台 |
| **dining car** | *can che* (tsan cher) 餐车 |
| **transfer** | *dao / huan* (dow / hwahn) 倒 / 换 |
| **get on (board)** | *shang che* (shahng cher) 上车 |
| **get off (disembark)** | *xia / shangche* (she-ah / shahng-cher) 下 / 上车 |

**Where is the train station?**
*Che zhan zai nali?* (Cher jahn zigh nah-lee) 车站在那里?

**Where is the ticket office?**
*Nali shi shou piao chu?* (Nah-lee shr show pee-ow choo) 那里是售票处?

**I want to go to____**
*Wo yao qu* ____ (Woh yow chwee____) 我要去 ____

**What is the track number?**
*Ji how huoche?* (Jee how hwoh-cher) 几号火车?

### What is the track number for Beijing?

*Qu Beijing zai ji hao tai?* (Chwee Beijing zigh jee how tie) 去北京在几号台?

### How do I get to the train station?

*Dao huoche zhan zenme zou?* (Dow hwoh-cher jahn zern-mo dzow) 到火车站怎么走?

### Please take me to the train station

*Qing dai wo dao huoche zhan* (Cheeng die woh dow hwoh-cher jahn) 请带我到火车站

### Do you have a railway timetable, please?

*Qing gei wo yige huoche shikebiao?* (Cheeng gay woh ee-guh hwoh-cher shr-ker-beow) 请给我一个火车时刻表?

### When does the train leave for Shanghai?

*Qu Shanghai de huoche jidian kai?* (Chwee Shang-hai der hwoh-cher jee-dee-an kigh) 去上海的火车几点开?

### Where do I buy a ticket?

*Piao zai nar mai?* (Pee-ow dzigh nah-urr my) 票在那儿买?

### Do I have to transfer anywhere?

*Wo jiang zai nali huanche?* (Woh jee-ahng zigh nah-lee hwan-cher) 我将在那儿换车?

## 39 Walk/Stroll Zou (dzow) 走 / Sanbu (Sahn-boo) 散步

### Let's go for a stroll

*Wo men qu sanbu* (Woh-mern chwee sahn-boo)
我们去散步

### I prefer to walk

*Wo xihuan zou-lu* (Woh she-hwahn dzow-loo)
我喜欢走路

**Is it too far to walk?**
*Zou lu qu tai yuan-le ma?* (Dzow loo chwee tie ywahn-ler ma) 走路去太远了吗?

**Can I walk there from the hotel?**
*Wo neng cong luguan zou qu ma?* (Woh nerng tsohng lwee-gwahn dzow chwee mah) 我能从旅馆走去吗?

## 40 Hotel *Luguan* (Lwee-gwahn) 旅馆
*Fandian* (Fahn-dee-an) 饭店

| | |
|---|---|
| **reservations** | *yuding* (yuu-deeng) 预定 |
| **reservations desk** | *Yuding chu* (Yuu-deeng choo) 预定处 |
| **hotel concierege** | *jiedaiyuan* (jeh-die-ywahn) 接待员 |
| **service fee** | *fuwu fei* (foo-woo fay) 服务费 |

**I have a reservation**
*Wo yijing yuding le fangjian* (Woh ee-jeeng yuu-deeng-ler fahng-jee-an) 我已经预定了房间

**I will be staying for two nights**
*Wo yao zhu liang tian* (Woh yow joo lee-ahng tee-an) 我要住两天

**I don't have a reservation**
*Wo mei you yuding* (Woh may you yuu-deeng) 我没有预订

**Do you any a/any vacancies?**
*You kong fangjian ma?* (You kohng fahng-jee-an mah) 有空房间吗?

**I would like it for two nights**
*Wo xiangyao zhu liang ye* (Woh she-ahng-yow joo lee-ahng yeh) 我想要住两夜

## I would like a room with a view

*Wo yao hao fengjing* (Woh yee-aw how ferng jeeng how)
我要好风景

## How much is the room rate?

*Fang fei duoshao qian?* (Fahng fay dwoh-shou chee-an)
房费多少钱?

## What time is breakfast?

*Jidian chi zaofan?* (Jee-dee-an chr dzow-fahn)
几点吃早饭?

## Do you have English language newspapers?

*Nimen zhe you mei you Yingwen baozhi?*
(Nee-mern jr you may you Eeng-wern bow-jr)
你们这有没有英文报纸?

## Where can I buy an English newspaper?

*Dao nar qu mai Yingwen baozhi?* (Dow nar-chwee my
Eeng-wern baow-jr) 到那去买英文报纸?

## Where can I get a map?

*Nar you ditu?* (Nah-urr you dee-too) 那有地图?

## Where can I buy an umbrella?

*Dao nar qu mai yusan?* (Dow nah-urr chwee my yuu-
sahn) 到那去买雨伞?

## I've lost my key

*Wo diu le wo de yaoshi* (Woh deo ler woh der yow-shr)
我丢了我的钥匙

## What time is check out?

*Shenme shijian tuifang?* (Shern-mo shr-jee-an tway-
fahng) 什么时间退房?

## Is there a service fee?

*You fuwu fei ma?* (You foo-woo fay mah) 有服务费吗?

**41** **Room Service** *Kefang yongcan fuwubu*
(Ker-fahng yohng-tsahn foo-woo-boo)
客房用餐服务部

### I would like to order breakfast

*Wo xiang dinggou zaocan* (Woh she-ahng deeng-gow
dzow-tsahn) 我想订购早餐

### Do you serve (have) Western food?

*You xi can ma?* (You she tsahn mah) 有西餐吗？

### Do you have Japanese food?

*You riben liao-li ma?* (You ree-bern lee-ow-lee mah)
有日本料理吗？

### Please bring me some scrambled eggs and toast

*Qing na chao jidan he kao mianbao gei wo*
(Cheeng nah chow jee-dahn her kow mee-an-bow gay
woh) 请拿炒鸡蛋和面包给我

**42** **Numbers** *Haoma* (How-oh-mah) 号码

### The Cardinal Numbers

  0 *ling* (leeng) 零
  1 *yi* (ee)* 一
  2 *er* (urr) 二; also liang (lee-ahng) 两
  3 *san* (sahn) 三
  4 *si* (suh) 四
  5 *wu* (woo) 五
  6 *liu* (leo) 六
  7 *qi* (chee) 七
  8 *ba* (bah) 八
  9 *jiu* (jeo) 九
 10 *shi* (shr) 十

*The pronunciation of *yi* changes to *yao* (yow) when used
in higher numbers.

From 10 on, the numbers are combinations of the first ten numbers. Eleven is 10 and 1, 12 is 10 and 2, etc. Twenty is 2-10; 30 is 3-10, and so on.

**11** *shiyi* (shr-ee) 十一
**12** *shier* (shr-urr) 十二
**13** *shisan* (shr-sahn) 十三
**14** *shisi* (shr-suh) 十四
**15** *shiwu* (shr-woo) 十五
**16** *shiliu* (shr-leo) 十六
**17** *shiqi* (shr-chee) 十七
**18** *shiba* (shr-bah) 十八
**19** *shijiu* (shr-jeo) 十九
**20** *ershi* (urr-shr) 二十
**21** *ershiyi* (urr-shr-ee) 二十一
**22** *ershier* (urr-shr-urr) 二十二
**23** *ershisan* (urr-shr-sahn) 二十三
**24** *ershisi* (urr-shr-suh) 二十四
**25** *ershiwu* (urr-shr-woo) 二十五
**26** *ershiliù* (urr-shr-leo) 二十六
**27** *ershiqi* (urr-shr-chee) 二十七
**28** *ershiba* (urr-shr-bah) 二十八
**29** *ershijiu* (urr-shr-jeo) 二十九
**30** *sanshi* (sahn-shr) 三十
**31** *sanshiyi* (sahn-shr-ee) 三十一
**32** *sanshier* (sahn-shr-urr) 三十二
**33** *sanshisan* (sahn-shr-sahn) 三十三
**34** *sanshisi* (sahn-shr-suh) 三十四
**35** *sanshiwu* (sahn-shr-woo) 三十五
**36** *sanshiliu* (sahn-shr-leo) 三十六
**37** *sanshiqi* (sahn-shr-chee) 三十七
**38** *sanshiba* (sahn-shr-bah) 三十八
**39** *sanshijiu* (sahn-shr-jeo) 三十九
**40** *sishi* (suh-shr) 四十
**41** *sishiyi* (suh-shr-ee) 四十一

**50** *wushi* (woo-shr) 五十
**60** *liushi* (leo-shr) 六十
**70** *qishi* (chee-shr) 七十
**80** *bashi* (bah-shr) 八十
**90** *jiushi* (jeo-shr) 九十
**100** *yibai* (ee-by)* 一百
**bai* is the designator for 100

**101** *yibailingyi* (ee-by-leeng-ee) 一百零一
**102** *yibailinger* (ee-by-leeng-urr) 一百零二
**103** *yibailingsan* (ee-by-leeng-sahn) 一百零三
**104** *yibailingsi* (ee-by-leeng-suh) 一百零四
**105** *yibailingwu* (ee-by-leeng-woo) 一百零五
**106** *yibailingliu* (ee-by-leeng-leo) 一百零六
**107** *yibailingqi* (ee-by-leeng-chee) 一百零七
**108** *yibailingba* (ee-by-leeng-bah) 一百零八
**109** *yibailingjiu* (ee-by-leeng-jeo) 一百零九
? — **110** *yibaishi* (ee-by-suhr) 一百十 *yibaiyishi*
**120** *yibaiershi* (ee-by-urr-shr) 一百二十
**130** *yibaisanshi* (ee-by-sahn-shr) 一百三十
**140** *yibaisishi* (ee-by-suh-shr) 一百四十
**150** *yibaiwushi* (ee-by-woo-shr) 一百五十
**175** *yibaiqishiwu* (ee-by-chee-shr-woo) 一百七十五
**200** *erbai* (urr-by) 二百
**201** *erbailingyi* (urr-by-leeng-ee) 二百零一
**300** *sanbai* (sahn-by) 三百
**400** *sibai* (suh-by) 四百
**500** *wubai* (woo-by) 五百
**600** *liubai* (leo-by) 六百
**700** *qibai* (chee-by) 七百
**800** *babai* (bah-by) 八百
**900** *jiubai* (jeo-by) 九百
**1,000** *yiqian** (ee-chee-an) 一千
**Qian* is the designator for 1,000.

**1,500** *yiqianwubai (ee-chee-an-woo-by)* 一千五百
**2,000** *liangqian (lee-ahng-chee-an)* 两千
**2,700** *liangquanqibai (lee-ahng-chee-an-chee-by)* 两千七百
**3,000** *sanqian (sahn-chee-an)* 三千
**4,000** *siqian (suh-chee-an)* 四千
**5,000** *wuqian (wuu-chee-an)* 五千
**10,000** *yiwan\* (ee-wahn)* 一万

*\*Wan is the designator for 10,000.*

**11,000** *yiwanyiqian (ee-wahn-ee-chee-an)* 一万一千
**12,000** *yiwanliangqian (ee-wahn-leeng-chee-an)* 一万两千
**15,000** *yiwanwuqian (ee-wahn-woo-chee-an)* 一万五千
**20,000** *erwan (urr-wahn)* 二万
**30,000** *sanwan (sahn-wahn)* 三万
**40,000** *siwan (suh-wahn)* 四万
**50,000** *wuwan (wuu-wahn)* 五万
**80,000** *bawan (bah-wahn)* 八万
**100,000** *shiwan (shr-wahn)* 十万
**150,000** *shiwuwan (shr-woo-wahn)* 十五万
**200,000** *ershiwan (urr-shr-wahn)* 二十万
**300,000** *sanshiwan (sahn-shr-wahn)* 三十万
**500,000** *wushiwan (woo-shr-wahn)* 五十万
**1,000,000** *yibaiwan (ee-by-wahn)* 一百万

## The Ordinal Numbers

The ordinal numbers are created by adding the prefix *di* (dee) to the cardinal numbers.

**1st** *diyi (dee-ee)* 第一
**2nd** *dier (dee-urr)* 第二
**3rd** *disan (dee-sahn)* 第三
**4th** *disi (dee-suh)* 第四

| | | | |
|---|---|---|---|
| 5th | *diwu (dee-woo)* 第五 |
| 6th | *diliu (dee-leo)* 第六 |
| 7th | *diqi (dee-chee)* 第七 |
| 8th | *diba (dee-bah)* 第八 |
| 9th | *dijiu (dee-jeo)* 第九 |
| 10th | *dishi (dee-shr)* 第十 |
| 11th | *dishiyi (dee-shr-ee)* 第十一 |
| 12th | *dishier (dee-shr-urr)* 第十二 |
| 13th | *dishisan (dee-shr-sahn)* 第十三 |
| 14th | *dishisi (dee-shr-suh)* 第十四 |
| 15th | *dishiwu (dee-shr-woo)* 第十五 |
| 20th | *diershi (dee-urr-shr)* 第二十 |
| 30th | *disanshi (dee-sahn-shr)* 第三十 |
| 50th | *diwushi (dee-woo-shr)* 第五十 |

**one half**    *yi ban (ee-bahn)* 一半
**one quarter**    *si fen zhi yi (suh fern jr ee)* 四分之一

## 43 Counting Things *Dongxi (Dohng-she)* 东西

The Chinese language uses special indicators, or "measure words," for counting things, based on what they are— people, flat things, round things, animals, fish, etc. There are over a dozen such terms, so keeping them straight, and using them properly, can be a problem for the beginner.

However, the most common of these indicators, *ge* (guh), can be used when you are uncertain about which one to use. The "measure words" go between the numbers and the nouns they apply to. Here is a list of the most common ones:

*ben* (bern) 本, used when counting books.

*ci* (tsu) 次, used when counting the number of times something occurs.

*ke* (ker) 棵, used when counting trees.

*suo* (swoh) 所, used when counting buildings and houses.

*tiao* (tee-ow) 条, used when counting large, long, slender objects like telephone poles.

*zhi* (jr) 支, used when counting small, round objects like pencils and sticks.

*zhang* (jahng) 张, used when counting flat things like pieces of paper.

*wan* (wahn) 碗, used when referring to bowls and things that come in bowls.

*ping* (peeng) 瓶, used for counting bottles and bottled things.

*kuai* (kwie) 块, used when referring to money.

*bei* (bay) 杯, used for counting glasses of water, etc.

**two bottles of beer**
*liang-ping pijiu* (lee-ahng-peeng pee-jeo) 两瓶啤酒

**three glasses of water**
*san-bei shui* (sahn-bay shway) 三杯水

**two hamburgers**
*liang-ge hanbaobao (lee-ahng-guh hahn-bow-bow)*
两个汉堡包

**one book**
*yi-ben shu* (ee-bern shoo) 一本书

**two sheets of paper**
*liang-zhang zhi* (lee-ahng-jahng jr) 两张纸

**I have three books**
*Wo you san-ben shu* (Woh you sahn-ben shoo)
我有三本书

**Pleave give me one sheet of paper**
*Qing gei wo yi-zhang zhi* (Cheeng gay woh ee-jahng jr)
请给我一张纸

**Two glasses of water, please**
*Qing gei liang-bei shui* (Cheeng gay lee-ahng-bay shway)
请给两杯水

**One hamburger, please**
*Qing gei yi-ge hanbaobao* (Cheeng gay ee-guh hahn-bow-bow) 请给一个汉堡包

## 44 Counting People *Ren* (wren) 人

| | |
|---|---|
| **people, person** | *renmin* (wren-meen) 人民 |
| **1 person** | *yi-ge ren* (ee-guh wren) 一个人 |
| **2 persons** | *liang-ge ren* (lee-ahng-guh wren) 两个人 |
| **3 persons** | *san-ge ren* (sahn-ge wren) 三个人 |
| **4 persons** | *si-ge ren* (suh-guh wren) 四个人 |
| **5 persons** | *wu-ge ren* (woo-guh wren) 五个人 |
| **6 persons** | *liu-ge ren* (leo-guh wren) 六个人 |
| **7 persons** | *qi-ge ren* (chee-guh wren) 七个人 |
| **8 persons** | *ba-ge ren* (bah-guh wren) 八个人 |
| **9 persons** | *jiu-ge ren* (jeo-guh wren) 九个人 |
| **10 people** | *shi-ge renmin* (shr-guh wren-meen) 十个人民 |

## 45 Time *Dian* (Dee-an) 点

Telling time in Chinese is a combination of the appropriate number, plus *dian* (dee-an), which means something like "point of time." In this usage it is the equivalent of the English "o'clock."

| | |
|---|---|
| **time (of day)** | *shijian* (shr-jee-an) 时间 |
| **hour** | *xiaoshi* (shee-ow-shr) 小时 |

| **half an hour** | *ban xiaoshi* (bahn-shee-ow-shr) |
| | 半小时 |
| **minute** | *fen* (fern) 分 |
| **a.m.** | *shangwu* (shahng-woo) 上午 |
| **p.m.** | *xiawu* (shee-ah-woo) 下午 |

In China the 24-hour day is divided into four periods:

| **midnight to 6 a.m.** | *qingzao* (cheeng-zow) 清早 |
| **(early morning)** | |
| **6 a.m. to noon** | *zaoshang* (zow-shahng) 早上 |
| **(morning)** | |
| **noon to 6 p.m.** | *xiawu* (shee-ah-woo) 下午 |
| **(afternoon)** | |
| **6 p.m. to midnight** | *wanshang* (wahn-shahng) 晚上 |
| **(evening)** | |

In designating the time period as well as the hour, both words precede the hour, as in the following examples.

| **1 a.m.** | *qingzao yi dian* (cheeng-zow ee dee-an) 清早一点 |
| **8 a.m.** | *zaoshang ba dian* (zow-shahng bah dee-an) 早上八点 |
| **1 p.m.** | *xiawu yi dian* (shee-ah-woo ee dee-an) 下午一点 |
| **8 p.m.** | *wanshang ba dian* (wahn-shahng bah dee-an) 晚上八点 |
| **what time?** | *ji dian?* (jee dee-an) 几点? |
| **at / in** | *zai* (zigh) 在 |
| **early** | *zao* (zow) 早 |
| **late** | *wan* (wahn) 晚 |
| **on time** | *zhunshi* (ju-wun-shr) 准时 |
| **in the morning** | *zai zaoshang* (zigh zow-shahng) 在早上 |
| **in the afternoon** | *zai xiawu* (zigh shee-ah-woo) 在下午 |

| | |
|---|---|
| **in the evening** | *zai wanshang* (zigh wahn-shahng) 在晚上 |
| **1 o'clock** | *yi dian* (ee dee-an) 一点 |
| **1 a.m.** | *zaoshang yi dian* (zow-shahng ee-dee-an) 早上一点 |
| **1:10** | *yi dian shifen* (ee dee-an shr fern) 一点十分 |
| **1:30** | *yi dian ban* (ee dee-an bahn) 一点半 |
| **2 o'clock** | *liang dian* (lee-ahng dee-an) 两点 |
| **3 o'clock** | *san dian* (sahn dee-an) 三点 |
| **2 a.m.** | *zaoshang liang dian* (zow-shahng lee-ahng dee-an) 早上两点 |
| **2 p.m.** | *xiawu liang dian* (shee-ah-woo lee-ahng dee-an) 下午两点 |
| **2:30** | *liang dian ban* (lee-ahng dee-an bahn) 两点半 |
| **3 o'clock** | *san dian* (sahn dee-an) 三点 |
| **3 a.m.** | *zaoshang san dian* (zow-shahng sahn dee-an) 早上三点 |
| **3 p.m.** | *xiawu san dian* (shee-ah-wuu sahn dee-an) 下午三点 |
| **3:15** | *san dian shiwufen* (sahn dee-an shr-woo-fern) 三点十五分 |
| **3:30** | *san dian ban* (sahn dee-an bahn) 三点半 |
| **4 o'clock** | *si dian* (suh dee-an) 四点 |
| **5 o'clock** | *wu dian* (woo dee-an) 五点 |
| **6 o'clock** | *liu dian* (leo dee-an) 六点 |
| **7 o'clock** | *qi dian* (chee dee-an) 七点 |
| **8 o'lock** | *ba dian* (bah dee-an) 八点 |
| **9 o'clock** | *jiu dian* (jeo dee-an) 九点 |
| **10 o'clock** | *shi dian* (shr dee-an) 十点 |
| **11 o'clock** | *shiyi dian* (shr-ee dee-an) 十一点 |
| **12 o'clock** | *shier dian* (shr-urr dee-an) 十二点 |

**What time is it?**
*Ji dian-le?* (Jee dee-an ler) 几点了?

**It is 6:30**
*Liu dian sanshi* (Leo dee-an sahn-shr) 六点三十

**It is 12:30**
*Shier dian sanshi* (Shr-urr dee-an sahn-shr) 十二点三十

**What time are we leaving?**
*Women shenme shijian zou?* (Woh-mern shern-mo shr-jee-an zoe) 我们什么时间走?

**What time does the bus leave?**
*Gonggong qiche ji dian likai?* (Gohng-gohng chee-cher jee-dee-an lee-kigh) 公共汽车几点离开?

**What times is breakfast?**
*Zaocan shi ji dian?* (Zow-tsahn shr jee dee-an)
早餐是几点?

**What times is lunch?**
*Wucan shi ji dian?* (Wuu-tsahn shr jee dee-an)
午餐是几点?

**What times is dinner?**
*Wancan shi ji dian?* (Wahn-tsahn shr jee dee-an)
晚餐是几点?

**One moment, please**
*Deng yi deng* (Derng ee derng) 等一等

**What time does the museum open?**
*Bowuguan jidian kaimen?* (Boh-woo-gwahn jee-dee-an kigh-mern) 博物馆几点开门?

**What time does the theater open?**
*Juchang jidian kaimen?* (Jwee-chahng jee-dee-an kigh-mern) 剧场几点开门?

**What time does the play start?**
*Huaju jidian kaishi?* (Hwah-jwee jee-dee-an kigh shr)
话剧几点开始?

**What time does the film start?**
*Dianying jidian kaishi?* (Dee-an-yeeng jee-dee-an kigh-shr) 电影几点开始?

## 46 Days *Tian* (Tee-an) 天

The days of the week, from Monday through Saturday, consist of the "day designator" *xingqi* (sheeng-chee) plus the numbers one through six. Sunday consists of the "day designator" plus *tian* (tee-an), the word for "day."

| | |
|---|---|
| **Monday** | *xingqiyi* (Sheeng-chee-ee) 星期一 |
| **Tuesday** | *xingqier* (Sheeng-chee-urr) 星期二 |
| **Wednesday** | *xingqisan* (Sheeng-chee-sahn) 星期三 |
| **Thursday** | *xingqisi* (Sheeng-chee-suh) 星期四 |
| **Friday** | *xingqiwu* (Sheeng-chee-woo) 星期五 |
| **Saturday** | *xingqiliu* (Sheeng-chee-leo) 星期六 |
| **Sunday** | *xingqitian* (Sheeng-chee-tee-an) 星期天 |
| **today** | *jintian* (jeen-tee-an) 今天 |

**What day is today?**
*Jintian shi xingqi ji?* (Jeen-tee-an shr sheeng-chee jee)
今天是星期几?

**Today is Monday**
*Jintian shi xingqiyi* (Jeen-tee-an shr Sheeng-chee-ee)
今天是星期一

| | |
|---|---|
| **every day** | *meitian* (may-tee-an) 每天 |
| **tomorrow** | *mingtian* (meeng-tee-an) 明天 |
| **tomorrow morning** | *mingtian shangwu* (meeng-tee-an shahng-woo) 明天上午 |
| **tomorrow** | *mingtian xiawu* (meeng-tee-an |

| | |
|---|---|
| **afternoon** | she-ah-woo) 明天下午 |
| **this morning** | *jintian zaoshang* (jeen-tee-an zow-shahng) 今天早上 |
| **this afternoon** | *jintian xiawu* (jeen-tee-an she-ah-woo) 今天下午 |
| **day after tomorrow** | *hou tian* (hoe tee-an) 后天 |
| **yesterday** | *zuotian* (zwoh-tee-an) 昨天 |
| **day before yesterday** | *qian tian* (chee an tee-an) 前天 |
| **in the morning** | *zai zaoshang* (zigh zow-shahng) 在早上 |
| **in the afternoon** | *zai xiawu* (zigh she-ah-woo) 在下午 |
| **in the evening** | *zia wanshang* (zigh wahn-shahng) 在晚上 |
| **last night** | *zuotian wanshang* (zwoh-tee-an wahn-shahng) 昨天晚上 |
| **early** | *zao* (zow) 早 |
| **late** | *wan* (wahn) 晚 |
| **on time** | *zhunshi* (joon-shr) 准时 |

# Counting Days

| | |
|---|---|
| **1 day** | *yi tian* (ee tee-an) 一天 |
| **2 days** | *liang tian* (lee-ahng tee-an) 两天 |
| **3 days** | *san tian* (sahn tee-an) 三天 |
| **4 days** | *si tian* (suh tee-an) 四天 |
| **5 days** | *wu tian* (woo tee-an) 五天 |
| **6 days** | *liu tian* (leo tee-an) 六天 |
| **7 days** | *qi tian* (chee tee-an) 七天 |
| **8 days** | *ba tian* (bah tee-an) 八天 |
| **9 days** | *jiu tian* (jeo tee-an) 九天 |
| **10 days** | *shi tian* (shr tee-an) 十天 |
| **21 days** | *ershiyi tian* (urr-shr-ee tee-an) 二十一天 |

**47 Weeks** *Xingqi* (Sheen-chee) 星期

**this week**       *zhei-ge xingqi* (jay-guh sheeng-chee)
                    这个星期
**last week**       *shang-ge xingqi* (shahng-guh sheeng-
                    chee) 上个星期
**next week**       *xia-ge xingqi* (she-ah-guh sheeng-
                    chee) 下个星期
**weekend**         *zhoumo* (joe-mwo) 周末
**week after next** *xiaxia-ge xingqi* (she-ah-shah-guh
                    sheeng-chee) 下下个星期

# Counting Weeks

**1 week**    *yi xingqi* (ee sheeng-chee) 一星期
**2 weeks**   *er xingqi* (urr sheeng-chee) 二星期
**3 weeks**   *san xingqi* (sahn sheeng-chee) 三星期
**4 weeks**   *si xingqi* (suh sheeng-chee) 四星期
**5 weeks**   *wu xingqi* (woo sheeng-chee) 五星期
**6 weeks**   *liu xingqi* (leo sheeng-chee) 六星期
**7 weeks**   *qi xingqi* (chee sheeng-chee) 七星期
**8 weeks**   *ba xingqi* (bah sheeng-chee) 八星期

**I will be in China for 2 weeks**
*Wo jiang zai Zhongguo dai liang-ge duo xingqi* (Woh
jee-ahng zigh Johng-gwoh die lee-ahng-guh dwoh
sheeng-chee) 我将在中国待两个多星期

**48 Months** *Yue* (Yuu-eh) 月

The Chinese word for month is *yue* (yuu-eh). *Yue* is used
when naming or listing the months, and *ri* (ree) is used when
giving dates. The names of the months consist of the
appropriate number plus *yue*—in other words, *yi* (one) plus
*yue* (month) equals January.

**January**           *Yiyue* (Ee-yuu-eh) 一月

| | |
|---|---|
| February | *Eryue* (Urr-yuu-eh) 二月 |
| March | *Sanyue* (Sahn-yuu-eh) 三月 |
| April | *Siyue* (Suh-yuu-eh) 四月 |
| May | *Wuyue* (Woo-yuu-eh) 五月 |
| June | *Liuyue* (Leo-yuu-eh) 六月 |
| July | *Qiyue* (Chee-yuu-eh) 七月 |
| August | *Bayue* (Bah-yuu-eh) 八月 |
| September | *Jiuyue* (Jeo-yuu-eh) 九月 |
| October | *Shiyue* (Shr-yuu-eh) 十月 |
| November | *Shiyiyue* (Shr-ee-yuu-eh) 十一月 |
| December | *Shieryue* (Shr-urr-yuu-eh) 十二月 |
| this month | *zhei-ge yue* (jay-guh yuu-eh) 这个月 |
| next month | *xia-ge yue* (shee-ah-guh yuu-eh) 下个月 |
| last month | *shang-ge yue* (shahng-guh yuu-eh) 上个月 |
| month after next | *xiaxia-ge yue* (shee-ah-shee-ah-guh yuu-eh) 下下个月 |
| monthly | *mei-ge yue* (may-guh yuu-eh) 每个月 |

To enumerate months, add the prefix *ge* (guh) to *yue*, the word for month, and put the appropriate number in front of the word:

| | |
|---|---|
| 1 month | *yi geyue* (ee guh-yuu-eh) 一个月 |
| 2 months | *liangge yue* (lee-ahng-guh-yuu-eh) 两个月 |
| 5 months | *wu geyue* (woo guh-yuu-eh) 五个月 |
| 6 months | *liu geyue* (leo guh-yuu-eh) 六个月 |
| 12 months | *shier geyue* (shr-urr guh-yuu-eh) 十二个月 |
| every month | *mei-ge yue* (may-guh yuu-eh) 每个月 |
| a few months | *ji-ge yue* (jee-guh yuu-eh) 几个月 |

**49** **Years** *Nian* (Nee-an) 年

| | |
|---|---|
| **this year** | *jin nian* (jeen nee-an) 今年 |
| **next year** | *ming nian* (meeng nee-an) 明年 |
| **last year** | *qu nian* (chwee nee-an) 去年 |
| **every year** | *mei nian* (may nee-an) 每年 |
| **one year** | *yi nian* (ee nee-an) 一年 |
| **two years** | *liang nian* (lee-ahng nee-an) 两年 |
| **three years** | *san nian* (sahn nee-an) 三年 |
| **four years** | *si nian* (suh nee-an) 四年 |
| **five years** | *wu nian* (woo nee-an) 五年 |
| **Happy New Year!** | *Xin Nian Hao!* (Sheen Nee-an How) 新年好! |
| **New Year's Day** | *Yuan Dan* (Ywahn Dahn) 元旦 |

**50** **Drink** *He* (Huh) 喝

| | |
|---|---|
| **coffee** | *kafei* (kah-fay) 咖啡 |
| **milk** | *niunai* (new-nigh) 牛奶 |
| **tea** | *cha* (chah) 茶 |
| **water** | *shui* (shway) 水 |
| **mineral water** | *kuangquan shui* (kwahng-chwahn shway) 矿泉水 |
| **ice** | *bing* (beeng) 冰 |

**I'm thirsty**
*Wo ke-le* (Woh ker ler) 我渴了

**What do you want to drink?**
*Ni xiang he shenme?* (Nee she-ahng her shern-mo) 你想喝什么?

**I'll have coffee, please**
*Qing lai kafei* (Cheeng lie kah-fay) 请来咖啡

**I'll have black coffee, please**
*Qing lai hei kafei* (Cheeng lie-ee-hay kah-fay) 请来黑咖啡

**More coffee, please**
*Qing duo lai kafei* (Cheeng dwoh lie kah-fay) 请多来咖啡

**I'll have green tea, please**
*Qing lai yi bei lucha* (Cheeng lie ee bay lwee-chah) 请来一杯绿茶

**Tea with milk, please**
*Qing lai yibei hongcha jia niunai* (Cheeng lie ee-bay hohng-chah jah new-nigh) 请来一杯红茶加牛奶

**I'll have tea with lemon, please**
*Qing lai yi bei ningmeng cha* (Cheeng lie ee bay neen-merng chah) 请来一杯柠檬茶

**More tea, please**
*Qing duo lai cha* (Cheeng dwoh lie char) 请多来茶

**A glass of milk, please**
*Qing lai yibei niunai* (Cheeng lie ee-bay new-nigh) 请来一杯牛奶

**Mineral water, please**
*Qing lai yibei kuangquan shui* (Cheeng lie ee-bay kwahng-chwahn shway) 请来一杯矿泉水

## 51 Bar *Jiuba* (Jew-bah) 酒吧

| | | |
|---|---|---|
| **beer** | *pijiu* (pee-jew) 啤酒 | |
| **draft beer** | *sanzhuan pijiu* (sahn-jwahn pee-jew) 山川啤酒 | |
| **black beer** | *hei pijiu* (hay pee-jew) 黑啤酒 | |
| **wine** | *putao jiu* (poo-tao-jew) 葡萄酒 | |
| **red wine** | *hong putao jiu* (hohng poo-tao-jew) 红葡萄酒 | |
| **white wine** | *bai putao jiu* (bigh poo-tao jew) 白葡萄酒 | |
| **martini** | *matini* (mah-tee-nee) 马丁尼 | |

| **whisky with soda** | *weishiji jia suda* (way-shr-jee jah soo-dah) 威士忌加苏达 |
|---|---|
| **whisky with water** | *weishiji jia shui* (way-shr-jee jah shway) 威士忌加水 |

**Let's go get a drink**
*Wo men qu he jiu* (Woh-mern chwee her jew) 我们去喝酒

**A glass of red wine**
*Yi bei hong putao jiu* (Ee bay hohng poo-tao-jew)
一杯红葡萄酒

**Two glasses of white wine**
*Liang bei bai putao jiu* (Lee-ahng bay bigh poo-tao-jew)
两杯白葡萄酒

**A bottle of beer, please**
*Qing lai yi ping pijiu* (Cheeng lie ee ping pee-jew)
请来一瓶啤酒

**Two bottles of beer, please**
*Qing lai liang ping pijiu* (Cheeng lie lee-ahng ping pee-jew) 请来两瓶啤酒

**A glass of beer, please**
*Qing lai yi bei pijiu* (Cheeng lie ee bay pee-jew)
请来一杯啤酒

**Draft beer, please**
*Qing lai yibei sanzhuan pijiu* (Cheeng lie ee-bay sahn-jwahn pee-jew) 请来一杯山川啤酒

**Two maotai, please**
*Qing lai liang bei maotai* (Cheeng lie lee-ahng bay mao-tie) 请来两杯茅台

**The bill, please**
*Qing jiezhang* (Cheeng jee-eh-jahng) 请结帐

## 52 Eat *Chi* (Chr) 吃

| | |
|---|---|
| **food** | *fan* (fahn) 饭 |
| | *can* (tsahn) 餐 |
| **Chinese food** | *Zhong can* (Johng-tsahn) 中餐 |
| **Western food** | *Xi can* (She tsahn) 西餐 |
| **restaurant** | *fanguan* (fahn-gwahn) 饭馆 |
| | *canguan* (tsahn gwahn) 餐馆 |
| **hotel restaurant** | *fan dian* (fahn dee-an) 饭店 |
| **dining room** | *can ting* (tsahn teeng) 餐厅 |
| **coffee shop** | *kafei ting* (kah-fay teeng) 咖啡厅 |
| **American-style breakfast** | *Meiguo zaofan* (May-gwoh zow-fahn) 美国早餐 |
| **menu** | *caidan* (tsigh-dahn) 菜单 |
| **rice (cooked)** | *mifan* (me-fahn) 米饭 |

**I'm hungry**
*Wo ele* (Woh uh-ler) 我饿了

**What do you want to eat?**
*Ni xiang chi shenme?* (Nee she-ahng chr shern-mo)
你想吃什么?

**Where shall we go to eat?**
*Wo men qu nali chi?* (Woh-mern chwee nah-lee chr)
我们去那里吃?

**What time do we eat?**
*Wo men shenme shi jian chifan?* (Woh-mern shern-mo
shr jee-an chr-fahn) 我们什么时间吃饭?

**Let's go eat**
*Rang wo men qu chifan* (Rahng woh-mern chwee chr-
fahn) 让我们去吃饭

**I like Chinese food**
*Wo xihuan Zhong can* (Woh she-hwahn Johng tsahn)
我喜欢中餐

**A table for two, please**

*liang wei* (lee-ahng way) 两位

**A menu (or menus), please**

*Qing na caidan* (Cheeng na tsigh dahn) 请拿菜单

**What is that?**

*Na shi shenme?* (Nay she shern-mo) 那是什么？

**I want that**

*Wo yao na-ge* (Woh yee-ow nay-guh) 我要那个

**Please give me** _____

*Qing gei wo* _____ (Cheeng gay woh _____) 请给我 _____

**Please bring me** _____

*Qing song* _____ *lai* (Cheeng sohng _____ lie)
请送 _____ 来

**I would like** _____

*Wo xiang yao* _____ (Woh she-ahng yee-ow _____)
我想要 _____

**More butter, please**

*Qing duo lai huangyou* (Cheeng dwoh lie hwahng-you)
请多来黄油

**Just a little, please**

*Jiu yidian dian* (Jew ee-dee-an-urr dee-an-urr)
就一点点

**Is that enough?**

*Na xie gou-le ma?* (Nah shay go-ler mah) 那些够了吗？

**Please give me a little more**

*Qing gei wo duo yidian* (Cheeng gay woh dwoh ee-dee-an) 请给我多一点

**That's enough!**

*Na xie gou-le!* (Nah shay go-ler) 那些够了！

**That's too much!**

*Na xie tai duo-le!* (Nah shay tie dwoh-ler) 那些太多了!

**I can't eat all of this!**

*Wo bu neng chi wan suo you-de!* (Woh boo nerng chr wahn swoh you-der) 我不能吃完所有的!

**53 Dim Sum\*** *Dian Xin* (Dee-an Sheen) 点心

\*This famous Cantonese dish (known virtually around the world) is called *dian xin* (dee-an sheen) in Mandarin, the national language.

**We want to eat dim sum**

*Wo men yao chi dian xin* (Woh-mern yee-ow chr dee-an sheen) 我们要吃点心

**I want to go to a dim sum restaurant**

*Wo yao qu dian xin fanguan* (Woh yow chwee dee-an sheen fahn-gwahn) 我要去点心饭馆

**I'm full!**

*Wo bao-le!* (Woh bow-ler) 我饱了!

**54 Peking Duck** *Beijing Kaoya* (Bay-jeeng Kow-yah) 北京烤鸭

**I'd like to have Peking Duck**

*Wo yao chi Beijing Kaoya* (Woh yee-ow chr Bay-jeeng Kow-yah) 我要吃北京烤鸭

**I want to go to a Beijing Duck restaurant**

*Wo xiang qu yige Beijing Kaoya guan* (Woh she-ahng chwee ee-guy Bay-jeen Kow-yah gwahn)
我想去一个北京烤鸭馆

**Is it very expensive?**

*Hen gui ma?* (Hern gwee mah) 很贵吗?

**I'd like to make reservations for dinner this evening**
*Wo yao ding jintian de wanfan* (Woh yee-ow deeng jeen-tee-an der wahn-fahn) 我要订今天的晚饭

**There will be three of us**
*Wo-men you san wei* (Woh-mern you sahn-wei)
我们有三位

## 55 Like / Don't Like *Xihuan* (She-hwahn) 喜欢
*Bu Xihuan* (Boo She-hwahn) 不喜欢

**I like it**
*Xihuan* (She-hwahn) 喜欢

**I don't like it**
*Bu xihuan* (Boo she-hwahn) 不喜欢

**I like Chinese food**
*Xihuan Zhong can* (she-hwahn johng tsahn) 喜欢中餐

**I'd like Western food**
*Wo xiang yao Xi cai* (Woh she-ahng yee-ow She tsigh)
我想要西餐

**It's delicious**
*Hao chi-de* (How chr-der) 好吃的

**It tastes good**
*Kekou* (Ker-koh) 可口

**I don't like Chinese food everyday**
*Bu xihuan meitian Zhong can* (boo she-hwahn may-tee-an Johng tsahn) 不喜欢每天中餐

## 56 Pay *Fuqian* (Foo-chee-an) 付钱

**bill / check**　　　　　*zhangdan* (jahng-dahn) 帐单

| credit card | *xinyong ka* (sheen-yohng-kah)<br>信用卡 |
| traveler's checks | *luyou zhipiao* (lwee-you jr-pee-ow)<br>旅游支票 |

### I want to pay the bill
*Wo yao fu zhang* (Woh yee-ow foo jahng) 我要付帐

### The bill, please
*Qing suan zhang* (Cheeng swahn jahng) 请算帐

### Separate checks, please
*Qing fenkai suan* (Cheeng fern-kigh swahn) 请分开算

### Do you take credit cards?
*Ni men shou xinyong ka ma?* (Nee-mern show sheen-yohng kah mah) 你们收信用卡吗?

### Do you take traveler's checks?
*Ni men shou luyou zhipiao ma?* (Nee-mern show lwee-you jr-pee-ow mah) 你门收旅游支票吗?

### A receipt, please
*Qing gei shouju* (Cheeng gay show-jwee) 请给收据

## 57 Have *You* (You)

### Do you have any / it / some?
*Ni you ma?* (Nee you mah) 你有吗?

### I have it / some
*You* (You) 有

### I don't have any / it
*Wo mei you* (Woh may you) 我没有

### Do you have the tickets?
*Ni you piao ma?* (Nee you pee-ow mah) 你有票吗?

**Do you have_____?**
*Ni you _____? (Nee you_____)* 你有 _____?

| | | |
|---|---|---|
| **boiled eggs** | *zhu jidan* (joo jee-dahn) | 煮鸡蛋 |
| **boiled water** | *kaishui* (kigh-shway) | 开水 |
| **bottle opener** | *kai ping qi* (kigh ping chee) | 开瓶器 |
| **a boyfriend** | *nan pengyou* (nahn perng-you) 男朋友 | |
| **a calendar** | *rili* (ree-lee) | 日历 |
| **a camera** | *zhaoxiangji* (Jow-she-ahng-jee) 照相机 | |
| **dim sum** | *dian xin* (dee-an sheen) | 点心 |
| **an envelope** | *xinfeng* (sheen-ferng) | 信封 |
| **a headache** | *touteng* (toe-terng) | 头疼 |

## 58 Don't Have *Mei You* (May Yoe) 没有

**I don't have my passport**
*Wo mei you huzhao* (Woh may you hoo-jow) 我没有护照

**I don't have any money**
*Wo mei you qian* (Woh may you chee-an) 我没有钱

**We don't have time**
*Wo men mei you shijian* (Woh-mern may you shr-jee-an)
我们没有时间

**I don't have an umbrella**
*Wo mei you yusan* (Woh may you yuh-sahn) 我没有雨伞

**I don't have a pen (ball point)**
*Wo mei you yuanzhubi* (Woh may you ywahn-joo-bee)
我没有圆珠笔

## 59 Telephone *Dianhua* (Dee-an-hwah) 电话

**local call**                    *bendi dianhua* (bern-dee dee-an-
hwah) 本地电话

| | |
|---|---|
| **long-distance call** | *changtu dianhua* (chahng-too dee-an-hwah) 长途电话 |
| **international call** | *guoji dianhua* (gwoh-jee dee-an-hwah) 国际电话 |
| **public telephone** | *gongyong dianhua* (gohng-yohng dee-an-hwah) 公用电话 |

### I want to make a phone call
*Wo xiang da dianhua* (Woh she-ahng dah dee-an-hwah)
我想打电话

### I want to make an international call
*Wo yao da yige guoji changtu dianhua* (Woh yee-ow dah ee-guh gwoh-jee chahng-too dee-an-hwah)
我要打一个国际长途电话

### I want to call long-distance
*Wo xiang da changtu* (Woh she-ahng dah chahng-too)
我想打长途

### May I use your phone?
*Wo keyi yong ni de dianhua ma?* (Woh ker-ee yohng nee der dee-an-hwah mah) 我可以用你的电话吗?

### A collect call, please
*Duifang fukuan* (Dway-fahng foo-kwahn) 对方付款

### What is your telephone number?
*Ni-de dianhua haoma shi?* (Nee-der dee-an-hwah how-mah shr) 你的电话号码是?

### My telephone number is _____
*Wo-de dianhua haoma shi* _____ (Woh der dee-an-hwah how-mah shr_____) 我的电话号码是 _____

### I want to send a fax
*Xiang da chuan zhen* (She-ahng dah chwan zhern)
想打传真

## 60 Cell Phone *Shou ji* (show jee) 手机

**Do you have a cell phone?**
*You shou ji ma?* (You show jee mah?) 有手机吗?

**I want to buy a cell phone**
*Wo yao mai shou ji* (Woh yee-ow my show jee)
我要买手机

**Where can I buy a cell phone?**
*Nali keyi mai shou ji?* (Nah-lee kuh-ee my show jee)
那里可以买手机?

**I want to rent a cell phone**
*Wo yao zu shou ji* (Woh yee-ow joo show jee)
我要租手机

## 61 Computer *Diannao* (Dee-an-now) 电脑
*Jisuanji* (Jee-swahn-jee) 计算机

| | |
|---|---|
| **computer hardware** | *yingjian* (eeng-jee-an) 硬件 |
| **computer software** | *ruanjian* (roo-an-jee-an) 软件 |
| **cord** | *dianxian* (dee-an-she-an) 电线 |
| **modem** | *tiaozhi jietiao qi* (tee-ow jr jay tee-ow chee) 调制解调器 |
| **hard disk** | *yingpan* (eeng-pahn) 硬盘 |
| **floppy disk** | *ruan cipan* (roo-an tsu-pahn) 软磁盘 |
| **mouse** | *laoshu* (lao-shoo) 老鼠 |
| **printer** | *dayin ji* (dah-een jee) 打印机 |
| **English word processing** | *Yingwen wenzi chuli* (Eeng-wern wern-dzu choo-lee) 英文文字处理 |

**I don't have a computer**
*Wo mei you jisuanji/diannao* (Woh may you jee-swahn-jee/dee-an-now) 我没有计算机 / 电脑

**May I use a computer?**
*Wo keyi yong diannao ma?* (Woh-ker-ee yohng dee-an-now mah) 我可以用电脑吗?

**I want to buy a disk holder**
*Wo xiang mai cipan jia* (Woh she-ahng my tsu-pahn jah) 我想买磁盘架

## 62 Internet / E-mail
*Yingtewang* (Eeng-ter-wahng) 应特网 /
*Dianzi youjian* (Dee-an-dzu you jee-an) 电子邮件

**I would like to check my email**
*Wo xiang cha wo-de dianzi youjian*
(Woh she-ahng chah woh-der dee-an-dzu you-jee-an)
我想查我的电子邮件

**Where can I go to get on the Internet?**
*Dao nali qu shang Yingtewang?* (Dow nah-lee chwee shahng Eeng-ter-wahng) 到那里去上应特网?

**Is there an Internet café?**
*You Yingtewang kafei dian?* (You Eeng-ter-wahng kah-fay dee-an) 有应特网咖啡店?

**I want to search the Internet**
*Wo xiang cha Yingtewang* (Woh she-ahng cha Eeng-ter-wahng) 我想查应特网

**How much is it per hour?**
*Yi-ge xiaoshi duoshao qian?* (Ee-guh shiaow-shr dwoh-shou chee-an) 一个小时多少钱?

**What is your email address?**
*Ni-de dianzi youjian xinxiang shishenme?* (Nee-der dee-an-dzu you jee-an sheen-she-ahng shr-shern-mo) 你的电子邮件信箱是什么?

## 63 Seasons *Jijie* (jee-jeh) 季节

| | |
|---|---|
| **spring** | *chunji* (chwun-jee) 春季 |
| **springtime** | *zai chuntian* (zigh chwun-tee-an) 在春天 |
| **summer** | *xiaji* (shee-ah-jee) 夏季 |
| **summertime** | *zai xiatian* (zigh shee-ah-tee-an) 在夏天 |
| **fall** | *qiuji* (chew-jee) 秋季 |
| **autumn** | *qiutian* (chew-tee-an) 秋天 |
| **winter** | *dongji* (dohng-jee) 冬季 |

### What is the best season in Beijing?
*Beijing-de nayi-ge jijie zuihao?* (Bay-jeeng-der nah-ee guh jee-jeh zway-how) 北京的那一个季节最好?

### When does spring begin?
*Chuntian shenme shihou kaishi?* (Chwun-tee-an shern-mo shr-hoe kigh-shr) 春天什么时候开始?

### Is it hot during the summer?
*Xiatian re ma?* (Shee-ah tee-an ruh mah) 夏天热吗?

### What is the best season in Shanghai?
*Shanghai-de nayi ge jijie zuihao?* (Shahng-high-der nah-ee guh jee-jeh zway-how) 上海的那一个季节最好?

### Does it get cold in Guangzhou in winter?
*Guangzhou dongtian leng ma?* (Gwahng-joe doong-tee-an lerng mah) 广州冬天冷吗?

## 64 Weather *Tianqi* (Tee-an-chee) 天气

| | |
|---|---|
| **temperature** | *wendu* (wern-doo) 温度 |
| **weather forecast** | *tianqi yubao* (tee-an-chee yuu-bow) 天气预报 |

### How is the weather today?
*Jintian tianqi zenmeyang?* (Jeen-tee-an tee-an-chee zen-mo-yahng) 今天天气怎么样?

63

### What is the temperature?
*Wendu you duoshao?* (Wern-doo you dwoh show)
温度有多少?

### Its cold!
*Man leng de!* (Mahn lerng der) 蛮冷的!

### Its hot!
*Man re de!* (Mahn ruh der) 蛮热的!

### It's sunny
*You taiyang* (You tie-yahng) 有太阳

### It's bad
*Bu hao* (Boo how) 不好

### It's windy
*You feng* (You ferng) 有风

### It's windy!
*Feng da!* (Ferng dah) 风大

### It's raining
*Xia yu le* (Shee-ah yuu ler) 下雨了

### It's snowing
*Xia xue le* (Shee-ah she-eh luh) 下雪了

## 65 Meet / Meeting *Jian* (Jee-in) 见 / *Hui* (Hway) 会

### Please meet me at my hotel
*Qing zai wo-de luguan zai jian* (Cheeng dzigh woh-der lwee-gwahn zigh jee-an) 请在我的旅馆再见

### What time shall I come?
*Wo shenme shihou lai?* (Woh shern-mo shr hoe lie)
我什么时候来?

**I'm sorry I'm late**
*Hen baoqian laiwan-le* (Hern bow-chee-an lie-wahn-ler)
很抱歉来晚了

**What time does the meeting start?**
*Hui-yi jidian kai shi?* (Hway-ee jee-dee-an kigh shr?)
会议几点开始?

## 66 Buy *Mai* (My) 买

**I want to buy _____**
*Wo xiang mai _____* (Woh she-ahng my_____)
我想买 _____

| | | |
|---|---|---|
| antiques | *gudong* (goo-dohng) 古董 | |
| apples | *pingguo* (peeng-gwoh) 苹果 | |
| bananas | *xiangjiao* (shee-ahng-jow) 香蕉 | |
| books | *shu* (shoo) 书 | |
| cashew nuts | *yaoguo* (yow-gwoh) 腰果 | |
| flashlight | *shoudiantong* (show-dee-an-tohng) 手电筒 | |
| jacket | *jiake* (jah-ker) 甲克 | |
| lacquerware | *qiqi* (chee-chee) 漆器 | |
| mineral water | *kuangquan shui* (kwahng-chwahn shway) 矿泉水 | |
| posters | *zhaotiehua* (jow-tee-eh-hwah) 招贴画 | |
| tea set | *chaju* (chah-jwee) 茶具 | |

**I would like an English-Chinese dictionary**
*Wo xiang yao yi ben Ying-Han zidian*
(Woh she-ahng yow ee-bern Eeng-Hahn dzu-dee-an)
我想要一本英汉字字典

**I want to buy a tourist map**
*Wo yao mai yi zhang luyou tu* (Woh yow my ee jahng lwee-you too) 我要买一张旅游图

**Shopping** *Maidongxi* (My-dohng-she) 买东西

| | |
|---|---|
| **shopping center** | *shangchang* (shahng-chahng) 商场 |
| **shop / store** | *shangdian* (shahng-dee-an) 商店 |
| **department store** | *baihuo shangdian* (by-hwoh shahng-dee-an) 百货商店 |
| **street market** | *shichang* (she-chahng) 市场 |
| **bookstore** | *shudian* (shoo-dee-an) 书店 |

## Where can I buy an umbrella?

*Nali keyi mai yusan?* (Nah-lee ker-ee my yuu-sahn)
那里可以买雨伞？

## Is there a department store near here?

*Zhe fujin you baihuo shangdian ma?* (Jur foo-jeen yoh by-hwoh shahng-dee-an mah?) 这附近有百货商店吗？

## What time do you open?

*Nimen shenme shihou kaimen?* (Nee-mern shern-mo shr-hoe kigh-mern) 你们什么时候开门？

## I want to go to a street market

*Wo yao qu shichang* (Woh yee-ow chwee shr-chahng)
我要去市场

## How much is this in US dollars?

*Zhe zhi duoshao Mei yuan?* (Jur jr dwoh-show May ywahn) 这值多少美元？

## I'm just looking

*Wo zhi kankan* (Woh jr kahn-kahn) 我只看看

## I'd like a raincoat, please

*Qing gei wo yuyi* (Cheeng gay woh yuu-ee) 请给我雨衣

## I'd like a pair of sandals, please

*Wo xiang mai liangxie* (Wo she-ahng my lee-ahng-shay)
我想买凉鞋

## I need some razor blades

*Wo xuyao guahu dao* (Woh shee yee-ow gwah-hoo dow)
我需要刮胡刀

## I need some sanitary napkins

*Wo xuyao yuejing dai* (Woh shee yee-ow yuu-eh-jeeng die) 我需要月经带

## I need some toilet paper

*Wo xu yao weisheng zhi* (Woh shee yee-ow way-sherng jr) 我需要卫生纸

## I am looking for _____

*Wo zai zhao* _____ (Woh zigh jow _____) 我在找 _____

## How much is this?

*Zhege duoshao qian?* (Jay-guh dwoh shou chee-an)
这个多少钱?

## How much is that?

*Na-ge duoshao qian?* (Nah-guh dwoh-shou chee-an)
那个多少钱?

## I want that

*Wo yao na-ge* (Woh yee-ow nah-guh) 我要那个

## May I have a receipt?

*Neng gei wo yige shouju ma?* (Nerng gay woh ee-guh show jwee mah) 能给我一个收据吗?

## Do you take US dollars?

*Nimen shou Mei yuan ma?* (Nee-mern show May ywahn mah) 你们收美元吗?

## Do you take British pounds?

*Nimen shou Ying bang ma?* (Nee-mern show Eeng bahng mah) 你们收英磅吗?

**Do you take travelers checks?**
*Nimen shou luyou zhipiao ma?* (Nee-mern show lwee-you jr-pee-ow mah) 你们收旅游支票吗？

**Do you take credit cards?**
*Nimen shou xingyong ka ma?* (Nee-mern show sheeng-yohng kah mah) 你们收信用卡吗？

## 68 Gifts *Liwu* (Lee-woo) 礼物

| | |
|---|---|
| **gift shop** | *lipin dian* (lee-peen dee-an) 礼品店 |
| **antique shop** | *gudong dian* (goo-dohng dee-an) 古董店 |
| **jewelry store** | *zhubao dian* (joo-bow dee-an) 珠宝店 |
| **bookstore** | *shudian* (shoo-dee-an) 书店 |

**Please show me _____**
*Qing gei wo kan _____* (Cheeng gay woh kahn _____)
请给我看 _____

**I want to buy _____**
*Wo yao mai _____* (Woh yee-ow my _____)
我要买 _____

**May I see that?**
*Wo keyikan na-ge ma?* (Woh ker-ee-kahn na-guh mah)
我可以看那个吗？

**May I look at it?**
*Wo neng kan ma?* (Woh nerng kahn mah) 我能看吗？

## 69 Cost/Price *Jiage* (Jah-guh) 价格

**Can you tell me the price?**
*Ni men neng bao yixia jiage ma?* (Nee mern nerng bow ee-shee-ah jah-guh mah) 你们能报一下价格吗？

**How much is this?**
*Zhe-ge duoshao?* (Jay-guh dwoh-shou) 这个多少？

**Is the price negotiable?**
*Keyi jiang jia ma?* (Ker-ee jee-ahng jah mah)
可以讲价吗?

**That one is too expensive**
*Na yi-ge tai gui* (Nah ee-guh tie gway) 那一个太贵

**70 Newsstand** *Baoting* (Bow-teeng) 报厅 / *Baotan* (Bow-tahn) 报摊

**Do you have (is there) a newsstand?**
*You baotan ma?* (You bow-tahn mah) 有报摊吗?

**Where is it?**
*Ta zai nali?* (Tah zigh nah-lee) 它在那里?

**Do you have English language newspapers?**
*You Yingwen baozhi ma?* (You Eeng-wern bow-jr mah)
有英文报纸吗?

**I'd like to buy this magazine**
*Zhe zazhi wo yao mai* (Jur zah-jr woh yee-ow my)
这杂志我要买

**I want to buy this book**
*Zhe shu wo yao mai* (Jur shoo woh yee-ow my)
这书我要买

**71 Post Office** *You Ju* (You Jwee) 邮局

| | | |
|---|---|---|
| mail | *you* (you) 邮 | |
| mail (verb) | *ji xin* (jee sheen) 寄信 | |
| mailbox | *youtong* (you-tohng) 邮筒 | |
| airmail | *hangyou* (hahng-you) 航邮 | |
| postage stamp | *you piao* (you pee-ow) 邮票 | |

**Where is the nearest post office?**
*Zuijin-de you ju zai nali?* (Zway-jeen-der you jwee zigh nah-lee) 最近的邮局在那里?

**How do I get to the post office?**
*Dao youju zenme zou?* (Dow you-jwee zern mo dzow)
到邮局怎么走？

**Please mail this**
*Qing ji zhe jian* (Cheeng jee jur jee-an) 请寄这件

## 72 Sightseeing *Guanguang* (Gwahn-gwahng) 观光

**I want to go sightseeing**
*Wo yao qu guanguang* (Woh yee-ow chwee gwahn-gwahng) 我要去观光

**I want to go to the Great Wall**
*Wo yao qu Chang Cheng* (Woh yee-ow chwee Chahng Cherng) 我要去长城

**How far is it?**
*Li zhe duo yuan?* (Lee jur dwoh ywahn) 离这多远？

**How long will it take?**
*Zhe yao duo chang?* (Jur yee-ow dwoh chahng?) 这要多长？

**Where is _____?**
_____ *zai nar?* (_____zigh nah-urr) _____ 在那？

**Can I walk there?**
*Wo keyi zou-lu ma?)* (Woh ker-ee dzow loo mah) 我可以走路吗？

**May we come in?**
*Keyi jinlai ma?* (Ker-ee jeen-lie mah) 可以进来吗？

**May I/we wait here?**
*Zhe keyi deng ma?* (Jur ker-ee derng mah) 这可以等吗？

**May I/we take photos here?**
*Zhe keyi zhaoxiang ma?* (Jur ker-ee jow-she-ahng mah) 这可以照相吗？

## 73 **See** *Kan* (Kahn) 看

**We want to see the Great Wall**
*Wo-men xiang kan Chang Cheng* (Woh-mern shee-ahng kahn Chahng Cherng) 我们想看长城

**Have you seen the Great Wall?**
*Ni kan guo Chang Cheng?* (Nee kahn gwoh Chahng Cherng) 你看过长城?

**We want to see Tiananmen Square**
*Wo-men xiang kan Tiananmen* (Woh-mern shee-ahng kahn Tee-an-ahn-mern) 我们想看天安门

## 74 **Travel Agent** *Luxing She* (Lwee-sheeng Sher) 旅行社

**We would like to see the downtown area**
*Wo men xiang qu kan shi zhongxin* (Woh-mern she-ahng chwee kahn shr johng-sheen) 我们想去看市中心

**Can you arrange a tour of the area?**
*Ni neng anpai bendi de tuyou ma?* (Nee nerng ahn-pie bern-dee der too-you mah) 你能安排本地的土游吗?

**How long is the tour?**
*Luyou yao duojiu?* (Lwee you yee-ow dwoh jew) 旅游要多久?

**Is it all right to take photographs?**
*Keyi zhaoxiang ma?* (Ker-ee jow-she-ahng mah) 可以照相吗?

## 75 **Martial Arts** *Wushu* (Woo-shoo) 武术

**I'd like to see a martial arts exhibition**
*Wo xiang kan wushu biaoyan* (Woh she-ahng kahn woo-shoo bee-ow-yahn) 我想看武术表演

**Where can I see a martial arts exhibition?**
*Wushu biaoyan zai nali?* (Woo-shoo bee-ow-yahn zigh nah-lee?) 武术表演在那里？

**Is there a fee?**
*You fei?* (You fay) 有费？

**How much is it?**
*Duoshao qian?* (Dwoh-shou chee-an) 多少钱？

## 76 Peking (Beijing) Opera *Jing Ju* (Jeeng Jwee) 京剧

**I want to go to the Beijing Opera**
*Wo yao qu kan Jing Ju* (Woh yee-ow chwee kahn Jeeng Jwee) 我要去看京剧

**What is on tonight?**
*Jintian wanshang shenme jiemu?* (Jee-an-tee-an wahn-shang shern-mo jeh-moo) 今天晚上什么节目？

**What is the name/ title (of the play)?**
*Jiao shenme mingzi?* (Jow shern-mo meeng-dzu) 叫什么名字？

**What time will it begin?**
*Shenme shihou kaishi?* (Shern-mo shr-hoe kigh-shr) 什么时候开始？

**Are the performers famous?**
*Yanyuan chuming ma?* (Yahn-ywahn choo-meeng mah) 演员出名吗？

**How long will it last?**
*Yan duochang shijian?* (Yahn dwoh-chahng shr-jee-an) 演多长时间？

**Where can I buy tickets?**
*Zai nali keyi mai-dao piao?* (Dzigh nah-lee ker-ee my-dow pee-ow) 在那里可以买到票？

**Is it necessary to buy tickets in advance?**
*Yiding yao tiqian mai piao ma?* (Ee-deeng yee-ow tee-chee-an my pee-ow mah) 一定要提前买票吗?

## 77 Emergency *Jinji qingkuang* (Jeen-jee cheeng-kwahng) 紧急情况

**I've lost my camera**
*Wo diule zhaoxiangji* (Woh dew-ler jow-she-ahng-jee) 我丢了照相机

**Someone has stolen my money**
*Renjia toule wo de qian* (Wren-jah tow-ler woh der chee-an) 人家偷了我的钱

**Someone has stolen my passport**
*Renjia toule wo de huzhao* (Wren-jah tow-ler woh der hoo-jow) 人家偷了我的护照

**Someone has stolen my purse**
*Renjia toule wo de qianbao* (Wren-jah tow-ler woh der chee-an-bow) 人家偷了我的钱包

**Help! (shout)**
*Jiu ming a!* (Jew-meeng-ah) 救命啊!

## 78 Ill/Sick *Bing* (Beeng) 病

**I'm sick**
*Wo bing le* (Woh beeng ler) 我病了

**I don't feel well**
*Wo gan jue bu hao* (Woh gahn-jway boo how) 我感觉不好

**It is very serious**
*Hen yanzhong* (Hern yahn-johng) 很严重

**I have a pain in my chest**
*Wo xiong teng* (Woh shee-ong terng) 我胸疼

**I have a pain in my stomach**
*Wo wei teng* (Woh way terng) 我胃疼

**I feel dizzy**
*Wo juede tou yun* (Woh jway-der toe ywun) 我觉得头晕

**I have a fever**
*Wo fashao-le* (Woh fah-shaow-ler) 我发烧了

**I have a heart condition**
*Wo you xinzang bing* (Woh you sheen-dzahng beeng) 我有心脏病

**I have diabetes**
*Wo you tangniao bing* (Woh you tahng-nee-ow beeng) 我有糖尿病

**I have a headache**
*Wo you dian toutong* (Woh you dee-an toe-terng) 我有点头痛

## 79 Medicine *Yiyao* (Ee-yee-ow) 医药

**drugstore (pharmacy)**   *yaofang* (yee-ow-fahng) 药房

**Where is a pharmacy?**
*Yaofang zai nali?* (Yee-ow-fahng dzigh nah-lee) 药房在那里?

**What time does the pharmacy open?**
*Yaofang jidian kai?* (Yee-ow-fahng jee-dee-an kigh) 药房几点开?

**I'd like some aspirin**
*Wo xiang yao asipilin* (Woh she-ahng yee-ow as-pee-leen) 我想要阿司匹林

### I'd like some eye drops
*Wo xiang yao yanyao shui* (Woh she-ahng yee-ow yahn yee-ow shway) 我想要眼药水

### I'd like something for a cold
*Wo xiangyao chi ganmao de yao* (Woh she-ahng-yee-ow chr gahn mao der yee-ow) 我想要吃感冒的药

### I'd like something for a cough
*Wo xiangyao chi kesou de yao* (Woh she-ahng-yee-ow chr ker-soh der yee-ow) 我想要吃咳嗽的药

### I'd like some contraceptives
*Wo xiang yao biyun* (Woh she-ahng yee-ow bee-ywun) 我想要避孕

**80** **Doctor** *Yisheng (Ee-sherng)* 医生
*Daifu (Die-foo)* 大夫

### I need to see a doctor
*Wo yao kan yisheng* (Woh yee-ow kahn ee-sherng) 我要看医生

### Is there a doctor who speaks English?
*You neng shuo Yingwen de yisheng ma?* (You nerng shwo Eeng wern der ee-sherng mah) 有能说英文的医生吗?

### Please call a doctor for me
*Qing gei wo jiao yisheng* (Cheeng gay woh jow ee-sherng) 请给我叫医生

### Call a doctor quickly!
*Gankuai jiao yisheng!* (Gahn-kwie jow ee-sherng) 赶快叫医生!

### Please prescribe Western medicine
*Qing gei wo Xiyao* (Cheeng gay woh She-yee-ow) 请给我西药

## 81 Dentist  *Yayi* (yah-ee) 牙医

**I have a toothache**
*Wo ya teng* (Woh yah terng) 我牙疼

**I've broken a tooth**
*Wo-de yachi duan-le* (Woh der yah-chr dwahn-ler)
我的牙齿断了

**I've lost a filling**
*Wo-de yatian liao diu le* (Woh der yah tee-an lee-ow
dew-ler) 我的牙填料丢了

**I need to go to a dentist**
*Wo yao qu kan yayi* (Woh yee-ow chwee kahn yah-ee)
我要去看牙医

**Can you recommend a dentist?**
*Ni jieshao yi-ge yayi hao ma?* (Nee jeh-shou ee-guh yah-
ee how mah) 你介绍一个牙医好吗?

## 82 Hospital  *Yiyuan* (Ee-ywahn) 医院

| | |
|---|---|
| Western hospital | *Xiyi yuan* (She-ee ywahn) 西医院 |
| emergency room | *jizhen shi* (jee-zhern shr) 急诊室 |
| accident | *shigu* (shr-goo) 事故 |

**Is there a hospital near here?**
*Zhe fujin you yiyuan ma?* (Jur foo-jeen you ee-ywahn
mah) 这附近有医院吗?

**Take me to a hospital**
*Song wo dao yiyuan qu* (Sohng woh dow ee-ywahn
chwee) 送我到医院去

**I want to go to a Western hospital**
*Wo yao qu Xiyi Yuan* (Woh yee-ow chwee she-ee ywahn)
我要去西医院

## 83 Ambulance *Jiuhuche* (Jew-hoo-cher) 救护车

**Please call an ambulance!**
*Qing kuai jiao jiuhu!* (Cheeng kwai jee-ow jew-hoo)
请快叫救护！

**It's urgent!**
*Hen ji!* (Hern jee) 很急！

**Take me (him/her) to the hospital!**
*Song wo (ta) dao yiyuan qu!* (Sohng woh (tah) dow ee-ywahn chwee) 送我(他)到医院去！

**She was hit by a car!**
*Ta bei qiche zhuangdao le!* (Tah bay chee-cher joo-ahng dow-ler) 她被汽车撞倒了！

## 84 Police *Jingcha* (Jeeng-chah) 警察

**"People's police"** *Renmin jingcha* (Wren-meen jeeng-chah) 人民警察
**police station** *jingcha ju* (jeeng-chah jwee) 警察局

**Call the police!**
*Kuai jiao jingcha!* (Kwai jee-ow jeeng-chah) 快叫警察！

**Someone has stolen my money**
*Renjia toule wo-de qian* (Wren-jah tow-ler woh-der chee-an) 人家偷了我的钱

**Someone has stolen my watch**
*Renjia toule wo-de shoubiao* (Wren-jah tow-ler woh-der show-bee-ow) 人家偷了我的手表

## 85 Embassy *Dashiguan* (Dah-shr-gwahn) 大使馆

**I want to go to the America Embassy**
*Wo yao qu Meiguo Dashiguan* (Woh yee-ow chwee May-gwoh Dah-shr-gwahn) 我要去美国大使馆

**I want to go to the _____**
*Wo yao qu* _____ (Woh yee-ow chwee _____) 我要去 _____

| | |
|---|---|
| **Australian embassy** | *Aodaliya dashiguan* (Ow-dah-lee-yah dah-shr-gwahn) 澳大利亚大使馆 |
| **Belgian embassy** | *Bilishi dashiguan* (Bee-lee-shr ....) 比利时大使馆 |
| **British embassy** | *Yingguo dashiguan* (Eeng-gwoh .....) 英国大使馆 |
| **Canadian embassy** | *Jianada dashiguan* (Jah-nah-dah .....) 加拿大大使馆 |
| **French embassy** | *Faguo dashiguan* (Fah-gwoh .....) 法国大使馆 |
| **German embassy** | *Deguo dashiguan* (Der-gwoh .....) 德国大使馆 |
| **Italian embassy** | *Yidali dashiguan* (Ee-dah-lee .....) 意大利大使馆 |
| **New Zealand embassy** | *Niuxilan dashiguan* (New-she-lahn ....) 纽西兰大使馆 |
| **Portuguese embassy** | *Putaoya dashiguan* (Poo-tou-yah .....) 葡萄牙大使馆 |
| **Spanish embassy** | *Xibanya dashiguan* (She-bahn-yah .....) 西班牙大使馆 |

## 86 Lost *Diu-le* (dew-ler) 丢了

| | |
|---|---|
| **lose (the way)** | milu (mee-loo) 迷路 |
| **lost (object)** | diu (dew) 丢 |
| **Lost-and-Found** | *Shiwu-Zhaoling-Chu* (Shr-woo Jow-leeng Choo) 事物招领处 |

**I'm lost**
*Wo milu-le* (Woh mee-loo-ler) 我迷路了
/uh

**I've lost my camera**
*Wo diu-le zhaoxiangji* (Woh dew-ler jao shee-ahng jee)
我丢了照相机

**I've lost my luggage**
*Wo diu-le xingli* (Woh dew-ler sheeng-lee) 我丢了行李

## 87 Barber Shop *Lifa Guan* (Lee-fah Gwahn) 理发馆

| | |
|---|---|
| **haircut** | *lifa* (lee-fah) 理发 |
| **shave** | *gua lian* (gwah lee-an) 刮脸 |
| **beard** | *huxu* (hoo-she) 胡须 |
| **massage** | *anmo* (ahn-moh) 按摩 |

**I want a haircut**
*Wo yao lifa* (Woh yee-ow lee-fah) 我要理发

**I want a shave**
*Wo yao gua lian* (Woh yee-ow gwah lee-an) 我要刮脸

**Please trim my beard**
*Qing xiu wo-de huxu* (Cheeng sheo woh-der hoo-she)
请修我的胡须

**Please massage my head**
*Qing anmo wo-de toubu* (Cheeng ahn-moh woh-der toe-boo) 请按摩我的头部

## 88 Beauty Parlor *Meirong Yuan* (May-rohng ywahn)
美容院

| | |
|---|---|
| **facial massage** | mianbu anmo (mee-an-boo ahn-moh) 面部按摩 |
| **haircut** | *lifa* (lee-fa) 理发 |
| **shampoo** | *xi tou* (she toe) 洗头 |
| **manicure** | *xiu zhijia* (show jr-jah) 修指甲 |
| **wash and blow dry** | *xi hou chuigan* (she hoe chway-gahn) 洗后吹干 |

**Is there a beauty parlor in the hotel?**
*Luguan you meirong yuan ma?* (Lwee-gwahn you may rohng ywahn mah) 旅馆有美容院吗?

**I'd like to make an appointment for tomorrow**
*Wo xiang yuding zai mingtian* (Woh she-ahng yuu-deeng dzigh meeng-tee-an) 我想预定在明天

**Please give me a permanent**
*Qing wei wo tang toufa* (Cheeng way woh tahng toe-fah) 请为我烫头发

**Please give me a shampoo**
*Qing wei wo xi tou* (Cheeng way woh she toe) 请为我洗头

## 89 Student *Xuesheng* (Shway-sherng) 学生

**I'm a student**
*Wo shi xuesheng* (Woh shr shway-sherng) 我是学生

**Here is my student card**
*Zhe shi wo-de xuesheng zheng* (Jur shr woh-der shway-sherng zherng) 这是我的学生证

**Can you give me a discount?**
*Neng da zhekou ma?* (Nerng dah juh-koe mah) 能打折扣吗?

ALSO MEANS "LOOK AT"

## 90 Read *Kan* (kahn) 看; *Du* (Doo) 读

**I cannot read Chinese**
*Wo bu hui kan Zhongwen* (Woh boo hway kahn Johng-wern) 我不会看中文

**Please read it to me**
*Qing du zhe-ge gei wo* (Cheeng doo jur-guh gay woh) 请读这个给我

**Please read it out loud**
*Qing da sheng du* (Cheeng dah sherng doo) 请大声读

**Can you read English?**
*Ni neng du Yingwen ma?* (Nee nerng doo Eeng-wern)
你能读英文吗?

**Can you read Romanized Chinese?**
*Ni neng du pinyin ma?* (Nee nerng doo Peen Een mah)
你能读拼音吗?

**91 Mistake**
*Cuowu* (Tswoh-woo) 错误 / *Cuoshi* (Tswoh-shr) 错事

**Excuse me, I think I made a mistake**
*Duibuqi, wo zuo-le yijian cuoshi*
(Dway-boo-chee, woh zwoh-ler ee-jee-an tswoh-shr)
对不起, 我做了一件错事

**Excuse me, I think you made a mistake**
*Duibuqi, ni zuo-le yijian cuoshi* (Dway-boo-chee nee
zwoh-ler ee-jee-an tswoh-shr) 对不起, 你做了一件错事

**He made a mistake**
*Ta zuo-le yijian cuoshi* (Tah zwoh-ler ee-jee-an tswoh-shr) 他做了一件错事

**That is not a mistake**
*Neige bu shi cuoshi* (Nay-guh boo shr tswoh-shr)
那个不是错事

**It is (there is) a big mistake!**
*You da cuoshi!* (You dah tswoh-shr) 有大错事!

**92 Rest** *Xiuxi* (Show-she) 休息

**I want to rest**
*Wo yao xiuxi* (Woh yee-ow show-she) 我要休息

**I need to rest**

*Wo xuyao xiuxi* (Woh she-yee-ow show-she) 我需要休息

**Can we rest?**

*Wo-men neng xiuxi ma?* (Woh-mern nerng show-she mah) 我们能休息吗?

**93 Rent** *Zu* (Joo) 租

**I want to rent a car**

*Wo yao zu yi liang che* (Woh yee-ow joo ee lee-ahng cher) 我要租一辆车

**What is the rate per day?**

*Meitian zu jin duoshao?* (May-tee-an joo jeen dwoh-shou) 每天租金多少?

**How do you charge for extra mileage?**

*Chaochu de licheng zenme suan?* (Chow-choo der lee-cherng zern-mo swahn) 超出的里程怎么算?

**Does the price include gasoline?**

*Jiaqian baokuo qiyou fei ma?* (Jah-chee-an bow-kwoh che-you fay mah) 价钱包括汽油费吗?

**I want an American car**

*Wo xiang yao yiliang Meiguo che* (Woh shee-ahng yee-ow ee-lee-ahng May-gwoh cher) 我想要一辆美国车

**How many kilometers are included in the basic fee?**

*Meitian jiben de gonglishu shi duoshao?* (May-tee-an jee-bern der gohng-lee-shoo shr dwoh-shou) 每天基本的公里数是多少?

**94 Bicycle** *Zixingche* (Jee-sheeng-cher) 自行车

**I want to rent a bicycle**

*Wo yao zu yi liang zixingche* (Woh yee-ow joo ee lee-ahng jee-sheeng-cher) 我要租一辆自行车

**What is the charge per hour?**
*Yi xiaoshi duoshao qian* (Ee she-ow-shr dwoh-shou chee-an) 一小时多少钱

**Do I have to pay in advance?**
*Yao xian fuqian ma?* (Yee-ow shee-an foo chee-an ma) 要先付钱吗?

**95 Street** *Jie* (Jeh) 街 / *Jiedao* (Jeh-dow) 街道

**alley (narrow street)** *hutong* (hoo-tohng) 胡同

**What is (the name of) this street?**
*Zhe shi neitiao jie?* (Jur shr nay-tee-ow jeh)
这是哪条街?

**96 Directions** *Fangxiang* (Fahng-she-ahng) 方向

**How do I get to _____?**
*Dao _____ zenme zou?* (Dow _____ zern-mo dzow)
到 _____ 怎么走?

| | |
|---|---|
| **the bus station** | *qiche zhan* (chee-cher jahn) 汽车站 |
| **the bus stop** | *qiche zhan* (chee-cher jahn) 汽车站 |
| **downtown area** | *chengli* (cherng-lee) 城里 |
| **the hospital** | *yiyuan* (yee-ywahn) 医院 |
| **the hotel** | *luguan* (lwee-gwahn) 旅馆 |
| **the post office** | *you ju* (you-jwee) 邮局 |
| **public market** | *shichang* (shr-chahng) 市场 |
| **railway station** | *huoche zhan* (hwoh-cher jahn) 火车站 |

**97 Books** *Shu* (Shoo) 书

**bookstore** *shudian* (shoo-dee-an) 书店

### I'm looking for books about China

*Wo yao zhao you guanyu Zhongguo de shu* (Woh yee-ow jow you gwahn-yuu Johng-gwoh der shoo)
我要找有关于中国的书

### I want to buy some books about China

*Wo yao mai guanyu Zhongguo de shu* (Woh yee-ow my gwahn-yuu Johng-gwoh der shoo) 我要买关于中国的书

### Where will I find books about the Chinese language?

*Nali you xue Zhongwen de shu?* (Nah-lee yee-ow shu-eh Johng wern der shoo) 那里有学中文的书?

### Where will I find guidebooks?

*Nali you luyou xiaoce?* (Nah-lee you lwee-you shou-tser) 那里有旅游小册?

## 98 Business *Shengyi* (Sherng-ee) 生意

| | |
|---|---|
| advisor | *guwen* (goo-wern) 顾问 |
| business person | *shangren* (shahng-wren) 商人 |
| business hours | *yingye shijian* (eeng-yeh shr-jee-an) 营业时间 |
| capital | *zijin* (dzu-jeen) 资金 |
| company | *gongsi* (gohng-suh) 公司 |
| conference meeting | *huiyi* (hway-ee) 会议 |
| conference room | *huiyi shi* (hway-ee shr) 会议室 |
| consulting company | *zixun gongsi* (zhe-sheen gohng-suh) 咨询公司 |
| contract | *hetong* (her-tohng) 合同 |
| director | *dongshi* (dohng-shr) 董事 |
| distributor | *xiaoshouzhe* (shee-ow-show-juh) 销售者 |
| general manager | *zong jingli* (zohng jeeng-lee) 总经理 |

| joint venture | *hezi qiye* (her-dzu chee-yeh) 合资企业 |
|---|---|
| office | *bangongshi* (bahn-gohng-shr) 办公室 |
| president | *zongcai* (zohng-tsigh) 总裁 |
| representative | *dailiren* (die-lee-wren) 代理人 |
| vice president | *fu zongcai* (foo zohng-tsigh) 副总裁 |
| foreign-own venture | *quanzi yongyou de waiqi* (chwahn-dzu yohng-you der wie-chee) 全资拥有的外企 |

### Where is your office?
*Nali shi ni-de bangong shi?* (Na-lee shr nee-der bahn-gohng shr) 那里是你的办公室?

### What time does the conference start?
*Huiyi jidian kai shi?* (Hway-ee jee-dee-an kigh shr) 会议几点开始?

## 99 Great Wall of China
*Chang Cheng* (Chahng Cherng) 长城

### We would like to see the Great Wall
*Wo men xiang qu kan Chang Cheng* (Woh-mern she-ahng chwee kahn Chahng Cherng) 我们想去看长城

### We want to go to the Great Wall
*Wo-men yao qu Chang Cheng* (Woh-mern yee-ow chwee Chahng Cherng) 我们要去长城

### Please take the most scenic route
*Qing zou fengjian hao de lu* (Cheen dzow ferng-jee-in how der loo) 请走风景好的路

### Can you wait for us?
*Ni neng deng wo men ma?* (Nee nerng derng woh-mern mah) 你能等我们吗?

### We expect to be back in two hours
*Wo men liang xiaoshi jiu huilai* (Woh-mern lee-ahng shee-ow-shr jew hway-lie) 我们两小时就回来

## 100 Goodbye

### Goodbye
*Zai jian* (Dzigh jee-an) 再见

### See you later
*Yi huier jian* (Ee hway-urr jee-an) 一会儿见

### We hope to see you again
*Xiwang wo men zai jianmian* (She-wahng woh-mern dzigh jee-an-mee-an) 希望我们再见面

# ADDITIONAL VOCABULARY

## China's Provinces

**Anhui** (Ahn-hway) 安徽
**Fujian** (Foo-jee-ahn) 福建
**Gansu** (Gahn-soo) 甘肃
**Guangdong** (Gwahng-dohng) 广东
**Guizhou** (Gway-joe) 贵州
**Hainan** (High-nahn) 海南
**Hebei** (Hub-bay) 河北
**Heilongjiang** (Hay-lohng-jee-ahng) 黑龙江
**Henan** (Her-nahn) 河南
**Jiangxi** (Jee-ahng-she) 江西
**Jilin** (Jee-leen) 吉林
**Liaoning** (Lee-ow-neeng) 辽宁
**Qinghai** (Cheeng-high) 青海
**Shaanxi** (Shah-ahn-she) 陕西
**Shandong** (Shahn-dohng) 山东
**Shanxi** (Shahn-she) 山西
**Sichuan** (Suh-chwahn) 四川
**Yunnan** (Ywun-nahn) 云南
**Zhejiang** (Jur-jee-ahng) 浙江

## China's Autonomous Regions

**Guangxi Zhuang** (Gwahng-shee Jwahng) 广西庄
**Nei Menggu** (Inner Mongolia) (Nay Merng-goo) 内蒙古
**Ningxia** (Neeng-shee-ah) 宁夏
**Xizang** (Tibet) (She-zahng) 西藏
**Xinjiang** (Sheen-jee-ahng) 新疆

# Major Cities in China

**Anshan** (Ahn-shahn) 鞍山
**Anyang** (ahn-yahng) 安阳
**Aomen / Macao** (Ow-mern) 澳门
**Baotou** (Bow-toe) 婦笋
**Beidaihe** (Bay-die-her) 北戴河
**Beihai** (Bay-high) 北海
**Beijing** (Bay-jeeng) 北京
**Changchun** (Chahng-chwun) 长春
**Changsha** (Chahng-shah) 长沙
**Chengde** (Chweeng-der) 承德
**Chungking / Chongqing** (Chohng-cheeng) 重庆
**Canton / Guangzhou** (Gwahng-joe) 广州
**Dali** (Dah-lee) 大里
**Dalian** (Dah-lee-an) 大连
**Daqing** (Dah-cheeng) 大庆
**Dunhuang** (Dwun-hwahng) 敦煌
**Foshan** (Fwo-shahn) 佛山
**Fuzhou** (Foo-joe) 福州
**Guangxi** (Gwahng-she) 广西
**Guangzhou / Canton** (Gwahng-joe) 广州
**Guiyang** (Gway-yahng) 贵阳
**Hainan** (High-nahn) 海南
**Harbin** (Hah-urr-bin) 哈尔滨
**Hohhot / Huhehaote** (Hoo-her-how-ter) 呼和浩特
**Hong Kong / Xianggang** (Shee-ahng Gahng) 香港
**Huang He** (Hwahng Her) 黄河
**Jilin** (Jee-leen) 吉林
**Jinan** (Jee-nahn) 济南
**Kaifeng** (Kigh-ferng) 开封
**Kunming** (Kwun-meeng) 昆明
**Mukden / Shenyang** (Shern-Yahng) 沈阳
**Lanzhou** (Lahn-joe) 兰州
**Lhasa** (Lah-sah) 拉萨
**Luda** (Loo-dah) 陆达

**Luoyang** (Lwoh-yahng) 洛阳
**Lu Shan** (Loo Shahn) 庐山
**Nanchang** (Nahn-chahng) 南昌
**Nanking / Nanjing** (Nahn-jeeng) 南京
**Nanning** (Nahn-neeng) 南宁
**Ningbo** (Neeng-bwo) 宁波
**Ningxia** (Neeng-shee-ah) 宁夏
**Qingdao** (Cheeng-dow) 青岛
**Qinghai** (Cheeng-high) 青海
**Qinhuangdao** (Cheen-hwahng-dow) 秦皇岛
**Quanzhou** (Chwen-joe) 泉州
**Qufu** (Chwee-foo) 曲阜
**Shanghai** (Shahng-high) 上海
**Shanhaiguan** (Shahn-high-gwahn) 山海关
**Shantou** (Shahn-toe) 汕头
**Shaoshan** (Shou-shahn) 韶山
**Shenzhen** (Shern-zern) 深圳
**Taiyuan** (Tie-ywahn) 太原
**Tianjin** (Tee-an-jeen) 天津
**Tulufan** (Too-loo-fahn) 吐鲁番
**Urumuqi** (Uu-roo-moo chee) 乌鲁木齐
**Wenzhou** (Wern-joe) 温州
**Wuhan** (Woo hahn) 武汉
**Wutai Shan** (Woo tie shahn) 五台山
**Wuxi** (Woo-she) 无锡
**Xiamen / Amoy** (She-ah-mern) 厦门
**Xian / Sian** (She-ahn) 西安
**Xinjiang** (Sheen-jee-ahng) 新疆
**Yanan** (Yahn-ahn) 延安
**Yangzhou** (Yahng-joe) 扬州
**Yixing** (Ee-sheeng) 宜兴
**Zhenjiang** (Jun-jee-ahng) 镇江
**Zhengzhou** (Juung-joe) 郑州
**Zhuhai** (Joo-high) 珠海

# Famous Places in Beijing

**Baiyun (Daoist) Temple**
*Baiyun Guan* (By-ywun Gwahn) 白云观

**Behai Park**
*Beihai Gongyuan* (Bay-high Gohng-ywahn) 北海公园

**Beijing University**
*Beijing Daxue* (Bay-jeeng Dah-shway) 北京大学

**Beijing Zoo**
*Beijing Dongwuyuan* (Bay-jeeng Dohng-woo-ywahn)
北京动物园

**Coal Hill**
*Jing Shan* (Jeeng Shahn) 景山

**Forbidden City**
*Zijin Cheng* (Dzu-jeen Cherng) 紫禁城

**Front Gate**
*Qian Men* (Chee-an Mern) 前门

**Gate of Supreme Harmony**
*Tai He Men* (Tie Her Mern) 太和门

**Great Hall of the People**
*Renmin Dahuitang* (Wren-meen Dah-hway-tahng) 人民大会堂

**Hall of Perfect Harmony**
*Zhong He Dian* (Johng Her Dee-an) 中和殿

**Hall of Preserving Harmony**
*Bao He Dian* (Bow Her Dee-an) 保和殿

**Hall of Supreme Harmony**
*Tai He Dian* (Tie Her Dee-an) 太和殿

**Hall of Union**
*Jiao Tai Dian* (Jow Tie Dee-an) 交泰殿

**Imperial Gardens**
*Yuhua Yuan* (Yuu-hwah Ywahn) 御华园

**Imperial Palace**
*Gu Gong* (Goo Gohng) 故宫

**Mao Zedong Memorial Mausoleum**
*Mao Zedong Jinian Tang* (Mao jer-dohng Jee-nee-an Tahng)
毛泽东纪念堂

**Marco Polo Bridge**
*Lugou Qiao* (Loo-go Chee-ow) 路沟桥

**Museum of Chinese History**
*Zhongguo Lishi Bowu Guan* (Johng-gwoh lee-shr Bwo-woo
Gwahn) 中国历史博物馆

**Museum of the Chinese Revolution**
*Zhongguo Geming Bowu Guan* (Johng-gwoh Guh-meeng Bwo-
woo Gwahn) 中国革命博物馆

**National Library**
*Zhongguo Tushuguan* (Johng-gwoh Tuu-shoo-gwahn)
中国图书馆

**Nationalities Cultural Palace**
*Minzu Wenhua Gong* (Meen-joo Wern-hwah Gohng) 民族文化宫

**North Lake Park**
*Beihai Gong Yuan* (Bay-high Gohng Ywahn) 北海公园

**Palace of Earthly Tranquility**
*Kun Ning Gong* (Kwun Neen Gohng) 坤宁宫

**Palace Temple**
*Yonghe Gong* (Yohng-her Gohng) 永合宫

**People's Cultural Park**
*Renmin Wenhua Gongyuan* (Wren-meen Wern-hwah Gohng-
ywahn) 人民文化公园

**Summer Palace**
*Yihe Yuan* (Ee-her Ywahn) 颐和园

**Temple of Heaven**
*Tian Tang* (Tee-an Tahng) 天堂

**Tiananmen Square**
*Tian An Men Guangchang* (Tee-an Ahn Mern Gwahng-chahng)
天安门广场

**Xidan Market**
*Xidan Shichang* (She-dahn Shr-chahng) 西淡市场

**Zhongshan Park**
*Zhongshan Gongyuan* (Johng-shahn Gohng-ywahn) 中山公园

# Famous Landmarks Near Beijing

**Great Wall of China**
*Chang Cheng* (Chahng Cherng) 长城

**Ming Tombs**
*Shi San Ling* (Shr Sahn Leeng) 十三陵

# Famous Shopping Districts in Beijing

*Jian Guo Men Wai* (Jee-an Gwoh Mern Wigh) 蒋国门外
*Liu Li Chang* (Leo Lee Chahng) 琉璃场
*Qian Men* (Chee-an Mern) 前门
*Wang Fu Jing* (Wahng Foo Jeeng) 王府井
*Xi Dan* (She Dahn) 西单

# Famous Places in Shanghai

**The Bund**
*Waitan Zhongshan Lu* (Wigh-tahn Johng-shahn Loo) 外滩中山路

**Fuxing Park**
*Fuxing Gong Yuan* (Foo-sheeng Gong Ywahn) 复兴公园

**Jade Buddha Temple**
*Yu Fosi* (Yuu Fwo-suh) 玉佛寺

**Longhua Temple & Pagoda**
*Longhua Miao he Ta* (Lohng-hwah Mee-ow her Tah) 龙华庙合塔

**Lu Xun Memorial Museum**
*Lu Xun Jinian Guan* (Loo-sheen Jee-nee-an Gwahn)
鲁迅纪念馆

**Museum of Natural History**
*Ziran Lishi Bowu Guan* (Dzu-rahn Lee-shr Bwo-woo Gwahn)
自然历史博物馆

**Old Town**
*Shanghai Jiu Shi* (Shahng-high Jew Shr) 上海旧市

**People's Park-Square**
*Renmin Guang Chang* (Wren-meen Gwahng Chahng) 人民广场

**Shanghai Acrobatic Theater**
*Shanghai Zajiyan Juyuan* (Shahng-high Zah-jee-yahn Jwee-ywahn) 上海杂技演剧院

**Shanghai Children's Palace**
*Shanghai Shaonian Gong* (Shahng-high Shou-nee-an Gohng)
上海少年宫

**Shanghai Exhibition Center**
*Shanghai Zhanlan Guan* (Shahng-high Jahn-lahn Gwahn)
上海展览馆

**Shanghai Museum of Art & History**
*Shanghai Bowu Guan de Yishu he Lishi* (Shahng-high Bwo-woo Gwahn der Ee-shoo her Lee-shr) 上海博物馆的艺术和历史

**Sun Yatsen Residence**
*Sun Zhongshan Guju* (Soon Johng-shahn Goo-jwee)
孙中山故居

**Tomb of Song Qingling**
*Song Qingling Fenmu* (Sohng Cheeng-leeng Fern-moo)
宋庆龄坟墓

**Worker's Cultural Palace**
*Gongren Wenhua Gong* (Gohng-wren Wern-hwah Gohng)
工人文化宫

**Xijiao Park**
*Xi Jiao Gong Yuan* (She Jow Gohng Ywahn) 西角公园

**Yu Garden**
*Yu Yuan* (Yuu Ywahn) 玉园

# Important Signs

| | |
|---|---|
| **Arrivals** | *Jinguan* (Jeen-gwahn) 进关 |
| **Departures** | *Chuguan* (Choo-gwahn) 出关 |
| **Customs** | *Haiguan* (High-gwahn) 海关 |
| **Bathroom** | *Yushi* (Yuu-shr) 浴室 |
| **Engaged** (toilet in use) | *Shiyongzhong* (Shr-yohng-johng) 使用中 |
| **Alley** (narrow street) | *Hutong* (Hoo-tohng) 胡同 |
| **Bicycle Parking** | *Cunche Chu* (Tswun-cher choo) 存车处 |
| **Bicycle Parking Zone** | *Zixingche Cunchechu* (Dzu-sheeng-cher Tswun-cher-choo) 自行车存车处 |
| **Car Parking Lot** | *Tingche Chang* (Teeng-cher Chang) 停车场 |
| **Closed Door** | *Guan Men* (Gwahn Mern) 关门 |
| **Business Hours** | *Yingye Shijian* (Eeng-yeh Shr-jee-an) 营业时间 |
| **Bus Stop** | *Qiche Zhan* (Chee-cher Jahn) 汽车站 |

| | | |
|---|---|---|
| **Caution** | *Xiaoxin* (Shee-ow-sheen) 小心 | |
| **Closed (business)** | *Tingzhiyingye* (Teeng-jr-eeng-yeh) 停止营业 | |
| | *Guanmen* (Gwahn-mern) 关门 | |
| **Danger** | *Weixian* (Way-shee-an) 危险 | |
| **Emergency Exit** | *Jinji Chukou* (Jeen-jee Choo-koe) 紧急出口 | |
| | *Taiping Men* (Tie-peeng mern) 太平门 | |
| **Entrance** | *Rukou* (Roo-koe) 入口 | |
| **Exit** | *Chukou* (Choo-koe) 出口 | |
| **Do Not Enter** | *Buxu Jinru* (Boo-shee Jeen-roo) 不许进入 | |
| **Don't Touch** | *Wuchu* (Woo-choo) 勿触 | |
| | *Wumo* (Woo-mwo) 勿摸 | |
| **Drinking Water** | *Yingyong Shui* (Eeng-yohng Shway) 饮用水 | |
| **Elevator** | *Dianti* (Dee-an-tee) 电梯 | |
| **Employees Only** | *Xianren Mianru* (Shee-an-wren Mee-an-roo) 闲人免入 | |
| **First Aid** | *Ji Jiu* (Jee Jeo) 急救 | |
| **Forbidden** | *Jinzhi* (Jeen-jr) 禁止 | |
| **Hospital** | *Yiyuan* (Ee-ywahn) 医院 | |
| **Information** | *Tongzhi* (Tohng-jr) 通知 | |
| **Information Desk** | *Wenxun Tai* (Wern-sheen tai) 问讯台 | |
| **Information Office** | *Wenxun Chu* (Wern-sheen choo) 问讯处 | |
| **Keep Out** | *Qie-wu Runei* (Chee-eh woo Roo-nay) 且勿入内 | |
| **Ladies' Room** | *Nu Cesuo* (Nwee Tser-swoh) 女厕所 | |
| **Left Luggage Storage** | *Xingli Jicun Chu* (Sheeng-lee Jee-tswun Choo) 行李积存处 | |
| **Luggage Lockers** | *Xingli Gui* (Sheeng-lee Gway) 行李柜 | |
| **Main Street** | *Dajie* (Dah-jee-eh) 大街 | |
| **Men's Room** | *Nan Cesuo* (Nahn Tser-swoh) 男厕所 | |
| **Non-potable Water** | *Fei Yingyong Shui* (Fay Eeng-yoong Shway) 非饮用水 | |

| | | |
|---|---|---|
| **No Entrance** | *Jinzhi Runei* (Jeen-jr Roo-nay) 禁止入内 | |
| **No Entry** | *Jinzhi Runei* (Cheen-jr Roo-nay) 禁止入内 | |
| **No Parking** | *Bu Xutingche* (Boo She-teeng-cher) 不许停车 | |
| **No Picture Taking** | *Qing Wu Pai-zhao* (Cheeng Woo Pie-jow) 请勿拍照 | |
| **No Smoking** | *Qing Wu Xiyan* (Cheeng Woo She-yahn) 请勿吸烟 | |
| **No Spitting** | *Qing Wu Tutan* (Cheeng Woo Too-tahn) 请勿吐痰 | |
| **No Trespassing** | *Buzhun Runei* (Boo joon Roo-nay) 不准入内 | |
| **Open (for business)** | *Yingye* (Eeng-yeh) 营业 | |
| **Open Door** | *Kai Men* (Kigh Mern) 开门 | |
| **Please Don't Touch** | *Qing Wu Dongshou* (Cheeng Woo Dohng-show) 请勿动手 | |
| **Please Line Up** | *Qing Paidui* (Cheeng Pie-dway) 请排队 | |
| **Police** | *Jingcha* (Jeeng-chah) 警察 | |
| **Public Bath** | *Yu Chi* (Yuu Chr) 浴池 | |
| **Public Telephone** | *Gongyong dianhua* (Gohng-yohng Dee-an-hwah) 公用电话 | |
| **Public Toilet** | *Gongyong Cesuo* (Gohng-yohng Tsuh-swoh) 公用厕所 | |
| **Pull** | *La* (Lah) 拉 | |
| **Push** | *Tui* (Tway) 推 | |
| **Reserved** | *Yuyue* (Yuu-yuu-eh) 预约 | |
| **Self-Service** | *Zi-Zhu* (Dzu-Joo) 自助 | |
| **Smoking Permitted** | *Keyi Xiyan* (Kuh-ee She-yahn) 可以吸烟 | |
| **Sold Out** | *Quan Man* (Chwahn Mahn) 全满 | |
| **Full House** | *Ke Man* (Ker Mahn) 客满 | |
| **Ticket Office** | *Shoupiao Chu* (Show-pee-ow Choo) 售票处 | |

| | |
|---|---|
| **Toilet** | *Cesuo* (Tser-swoh) 厕所 |
| **Vacancy** | *You Kong Fang* (You Kohng Fahng) 有空房 |
| **Waiting Room** | *Xiuxi Shi* (Sheo-she Shr) 休息室 |
| **Welcome** | *Huanying Guanglin* (Hwahn-eeng Gwahng-leen) 欢迎光临 |
| **Admission Free** | *Mianfei Ruchang* (Mee-an-fay Roo-chahng) 免费入场 |

# Other Countries in Chinese

| | |
|---|---|
| **Australia** | *Aodaliya* (Ah-oh-dah-lee-ah) 奥大利亚 |
| **Canada** | *Jianada* (Jya-nah-dah) 加拿大 |
| **France** | *Faguo* (Fah-gwoh) 法国 |
| **Germany** | *Deguo* (Duh-gwoh) 德国 |
| **Great Britain** | *Yingguo* (Eeng-gwoh) 英国 |
| **India** | *Yindu* (Een-doo) 印度 |
| **Italy** | *Yidali* (Ee-dah-lee) 意大利 |
| **Japan** | *Riben* (Ree-bern) 日本 |
| **Korea** | *Chaoxian* (Chow-she-an) 朝鲜 |
| **New Zealand** | *Niu Xilan* (New She-lahn) 纽西兰 |
| **Pakistan** | *Bajisitan* (Bah-jee-she-tahn) 巴基斯坦 |
| **Spain** | *Xibanya* (She-bahn-yah) 西班牙 |
| **United States** | *Meiguo* (May-gwoh) 美国 |

# Terms With Opposite Meanings

| | |
|---|---|
| **big / small** | *da / xiao* (dah / shaow) 大 / 小 |
| **heavy / light** | *zhong / qing* (johng / cheeng) 重 / 轻 |
| **long / short** | *chang / duan* (chahng / dwan) 长 / 短 |
| **good / bad** | *hao / huai* (how / hwai) 好 / 坏 |
| **cheap / expensive** | *pianyi / gui* (pee-an-ee / gwee) 便宜 / 贵 |
| **easy / difficult** | *rongyi / nan* (rohng ee / nahn) 容易 / 难 |
| **true / false** | *zhen / jia* (jun / jah) 真 / 假 |
| **quick / slow** | *kuai / man* (kwie / mahn) 快 / 慢 |

| left / right | *zuo / you* (zwoh / you) 左 / 右 |
| early / late | *zao / wan* (dzow / wahn) 早 / 晚 |
| old / young | *lao / shao* (lao / shaow) 老 / 少 |
| full / empty | *man / kong* (mahn / kohng) 满 / 空 |
| safe / dangerous | *anquan / wexian* |
| | (ahn-chwan / way-shee-an) 安全 / 危险 |
| quiet / noisy | *anjing / chaonao* |
| | (ahn-jeen / chow-now) 安静 / 吵闹 |
| inside / outside | *libian / waibian* |
| | (lee-bee-an / wie-bee-an) 里边 / 外边 |
| first / last | *xian / hou* (shee-an / hoh) 先 / 后 |
| before / after | *yiqian / yihou* |
| | (ee-chee-an / ee-hoh) 以前 / 以后 |

# Words A to Z

[A]

| Abacus | *suanpan* (swahn-pahn) 算盘 |
| abroad | *guowai* (gwoh-wigh) 国外 |
| accept | *jie shou* (jay show) 接受 |
| accurate | *zhunque* (joon-chueh) 准确 |
| actor | *yanyun* (yahn-ywahn) 演员 |
| acupuncture | *zhenjiu* (jun-jeo) 针灸 |
| adaptor plug | *zhuangjie qi* (jwahn-jee-eh chee) 转接器 |
| address | *dizhi* (dee-jr) 地址 |
| admission | *ruchang* (roo-chahng) 入场 |
| adult | *daren* (dah-wren) 大人 |
| aerobics | *jianmei cao* (jee-an-may tsow) 健美操 |
| after | *guo* (gwoh) 过 |
| again | *zai* (zigh) 再 |
| against | *fan dui* (fahn dway) 反对 |
| agree | *tongyi* (tohng-ee) 同意 |
| agriculture | *nongye* (nohng-yeh) 农业 |
| AIDS | *aizi bing* (aa-dzu beeng) 爱滋病 |
| air | *kongqi* (kohng-chee) 空气 |

| | | |
|---|---|---|
| airconditioned | *kongtiao* (kohng-tee-ow) 空调 | |
| air-conditioner | *kongtiaoji* (kohng-tow-jee) 空调机 | |
| airline (company) | *hangkong gongsi* (hahng-kohng gohng-suh) 航空公司 | |
| airline hostess | *kongzhong xiaojie* (kohng-johng shiaow-jah) 空中小姐 | |
| airline ticket | *feiji piao* (fay-jee pee-ow) 飞机票 | |
| air pollution | *kongqi wuran* (koong-chee woo-rahn) 空气污染 | |
| airsick | yunji (ywun-jee) 晕机 | |
| alarm clock | *nao zhong* (now johng) 闹钟 | |
| alcohol | *jiu* (jeo) 酒 | |
| a little | *yidian* (ee-dee-an) 一点 | |
| all | *quanbu* (chwahn boo) 全部 | |
| allergy | *guomin* (gwoh-meen) 过敏 | |
| alley | *hutong* (hoo-tohng) 胡同 | |
| altitude | *haiba* (high-bah) 海拔 | |
| ambassador | *dashi* (dah-shr) 大使 | |
| amount, total | *zong e* (zohng urr) 总额 | |
| amusing, fun | *haowanr* (how-wahn) 好玩 | |
| ancient | *gudai-de* (goo-die-duh) 古代的 | |
| angry | *shengqi* (sherng-chee) 生气 | |
| animal | *dongwu* (dohng-woo) 动物 | |
| anniversary | *zhounian jinian* (joe-nee-an jee-nee-an) 周年纪念 | |
| announcement | *gonggao* (gohng gaw) 公告 | |
| answer | *huida* (hway-dah) 回答 | |
| antibiotics | *kangshengsu* (kahng-sherng-soo) 抗生素 | |
| apartment | *danyuan fang* (dahn-ywahn fahng) 单元房 | |
| appendicitis | *mangchang yan* (mahng chahng yahn) 盲肠炎 | |
| appetizer | *lengpan* (lerng-pahn) 冷盘 | |
| applaud | *paishou* (pie-show) 拍手 | |

| | | |
|---|---|---|
| appliance | *diangqi* (dee-an-chee) | 电器 |
| application | *shengqing* (sherng-cheeng) | 申请 |
| application form | *shengqing biao* (sherng-cheeng bow) | 申请表 |
| appointment | *yuehui* (yway-hway) | 约会 |
| appreciate | *xinshang* (sheen-shahng) | 欣赏 |
| architecture | *jianzhu* (jee-an-joo) | 建筑 |
| area (district) | *yidai* (ee-die) | 一带 |
| army | *jundui* (jwin-dway) | 军队 |
| arrive | *daoda* (dow-dah) | 到达 |
| art | *yishu* (ee-shoo) | 艺术 |
| | *meishu* (may-shoo) | 美术 |
| art gallery | *hualang* (hwah-lahng) | 画廊 |
| artist | *yishujia* (ee-shoo-jah) | 艺术家 |
| art museum | *meishu guan* (may-shoo gwahn) | 美术馆 |
| arts & crafts | *gongyi meishu* (gohng-ee may-shoo) | 工艺美术 |
| Asia | *Yazhou* (Yah-joe) | 亚洲 |
| ask | *wen* (wern) | 问 |
| assignment | *gongzuo* (gohng-zwoh) | 工作 |
| assist, help | *bangzhu* (bahng-joo) | 帮助 |
| asthma | *qichuan bing* (chee-chwahn beeng) | 气喘病 |
| athletics | *yundong* (ywun-dohng) | 运动 |
| attorney | *lushi* (lwee-shr) | 律师 |
| attractive | *xiyinren* (she-een-wren) | 吸引人 |
| audience | *guanzhong* (gwahn-johng) | 观众 |
| auditorium | *litang* (lee-tahng) | 礼堂 |
| aunt | *gugu* (goo-goo) | 姑姑 |
| authentic | *kekao* (ker-kow) | 可靠 |
| author | *zuozhe* (zwoh-juh) | 作者 |
| authorize | *shouquan* (show-chwahn) | 授权 |
| automatic | *zidong* (dzu-dohng) | 自动 |
| automobile | *qiche* (chee-cher) | 汽车 |
| avenue | *dajie* (dah-jeh) | 大街 |

| | | |
|---|---|---|
| **average** | *pingjun* (peeng-jwin) | 平均 |
| **awake, wake up** | *huangxing* (hwahng-sheeng) | 唤醒 |

**[B]**

| | | |
|---|---|---|
| **baby** | *yinger* (eeng-urr) | 婴儿 |
| **baby food** | *yinger shipin* (eeng-urr shr-peen) | 婴儿食品 |
| **bachelor** | *danshenhan* (dahn-shern-hahn) | 单身汉 |
| **back door** | *hou men* (hoe mern) | 后门 |
| **back yard** | *hou yuan* (hoe ywahn) | 后院 |
| **bad quality** | *cha* (chah) | 差 |
| **bag** | *daizi* (die-dzu) | 袋子 |
| **baggage** | *xingli* (sheeng-lee) | 行李 |
| **baggage cart** | *xingli che* (sheeng-lee cher) | 行李车 |
| **baggage check** | *xingli tuoyundan* (sheeng-lee twoh-ywun-dahn) | 行李托运单 |
| **baggage claim** | *xingli ting* (sheeng-lee teeng) | 行李厅 |
| **baggage tax** | *xingli pai* (sheeng-lee pie) | 行李牌 |
| **bakery** | *mianbao dian* (me-an-bow dee-an) | 面包店 |
| **ball** | *qiu* (cheo) | 球 |
| **ball game** | *qiu sai* (cheo sigh) | 球赛 |
| **ballpoint pen** | *yuanzhu bi* (ywahn-joo bee) | 圆珠笔 |
| **ballroom** | *wuting* (woo-teeng) | 舞厅 |
| **bamboo** | *zhuzi* (joo-dzu) | 竹子 |
| **bamboo shoots** | *zhu sun* (joo soon) | 竹笋 |
| **banana** | *xiangjiao* (she-ahng-jow) | 香蕉 |
| **band (musical)** | *yuedui* (yway-dway) | 乐队 |
| **bandage** | *bengdai* (bung-die) | 绷带 |
| **band-aid** | *zhixue jiaobu* (jr-shway jee-ow-boo) | 止血胶布 |
| **bank** | *yinhang* (een-hahng) | 银行 |
| **banquet** | *yanhui* (yahn-hway) | 宴会 |
| **banquet room** | *yanhui ting* (yahn-hway teeng) | 宴会厅 |
| **bar (drinking)** | *jiuba* (jeo-bah) | 酒吧 |

| | | |
|---|---|---|
| barbecue | *kao* (kow) 烤 | |
| barter | *yihuo yihuo* (ee-hwoh ee-hwoh) 以货易货 | |
| baseball | *bangqiu* (bahng-cheo) 棒球 | |
| basement | *dixiashi* (dee-she-ah-shr) 地下室 | |
| basketball | *lanqiu* (lahn-cheo) 篮球 | |
| basketball game | *lanqiu sai* (lahn-cheo sigh) 篮球赛 | |
| bath | *yugang* (yuu-gahng) 浴缸 | |
| bathe | *xizao* (she-zow) 洗澡 | |
| bathing beach | *yu chang* (yuu chahng) 浴场 | |
| bathing suit | *youyongyi* (you-yohng-ee) 游泳衣 | |
| bathrobe | *yuyi* (yuu yee) 浴衣 | |
| bathroom (bath) | *yushi* (yuu-shr) 浴室 | |
| bathroom (toilet) | *cesuo* (tser-swoh) 厕所 | |
| bath towel | *xizao maojin* (she-zow mao-jeen) 洗澡毛巾 | |
| bathtub | *zaopen* (zow-pern) 澡盆 | |
| batteries | *dianchi* (dee-an-chr) 电池 | |
| bay | *haiwan* (high-wahn) 海湾 | |
| beach | *haitan* (high-tahn) 海滩 | |
| bean curd | *doufu* (doe-foo) 豆腐 | |
| beard | *huzi* (hoo-dzu) 胡子 | |
| beat, win | *ying* (eeng) 赢 | |
| beautiful | *piaoliang* (pee-ow-lee-ahng) 漂亮 | |
| beauty (natural) | *ziranmei* (dzu-rahn-may) 自然美 | |
| beauty salon | *fa lang* (fah lahng) 发廊 | |
| bed | *chuang* (chwahng) 床 | |
| bedroom | *woshi* (woh-shr) 卧室 | |
| | *wofang* (woh-fahng) 卧房 | |
| beef | *niurou* (new-roe) 牛肉 | |
| beefsteak | *niu pai* (new pie) 牛排 | |
| before | *yiqian* (ee-chee-an) 以前 | |
| bell (door) | *ling* (leeng) 铃 | |
| bell captain | *xingli lingban* (sheeng-lee leeng-bahn) 行李领班 | |

| | | |
|---|---|---|
| belt | *yaodai* (yee-ow-die) 腰带 | |
| best | *zuihao* (zway-how) 最好 | |
| better | *bijiaohao* (bee-jow-how) 比较好 | |
| big, large, great | *da* (dah) 大 | |
| birds | *niao* (nee-ow) 鸟 | |
| birth control | *jieyu* (jeh-yuu) 节育 | |
| birthday | *shengri* (sherng-rr) 生日 | |
| (of old person) | | |
| biscuit | *binggan* (beeng-gahn) 饼干 | |
| black | *hei* (hay) 黑 | |
| blanket | *tanzi* (tahn-dzu) 毯子 | |
| bleed | *liuxue* (lew-shway) 流血 | |
| blonde | *jinfa* (jeen-fah) 金发 | |
| blister | *pao* (pow) 疱 | |
| blood-pressure | *xueya* (shway-yah) 血压 | |
| blood type | *xue xing* (shway sheeng) 血型 | |
| blue | *lan* (lahn) 蓝 | |
| boarding pass | *dengji zheng* (derng-jee zherng) 登记证 | |
| boat | *chuan* (chwahn) 船 | |
| body (human) | *shenti* (shern-tee) 身体 | |
| body temperature | *tiwen* (tee-wern) 体温 | |
| boil (verb) | *zhu* (joo) 煮 | |
| boiled egg | *zhu jidan* (joo jee-dahn) 煮鸡蛋 | |
| boiled water | *kai shui* (kigh shway) 开水 | |
| bon voyage | *yilushunfeng* (ee-loo-shwern-ferng) 一路顺风 | |
| bookkeeper | *kuaiji* (kwie-jee) 会计 | |
| booth | *ting* (teeng) 亭 | |
| boots | *xuezi* (shway-dzu) 靴子 | |
| border | *bianjie* (bee-an-jay) 边界 | |
| borrow | *jie* (jay) 借 | |
| boss | *laoban* (lao-bahn) 老板 | |
| bottle | *ping* (peeng) 瓶 | |
| bottle opener | *kai pingqi* (kigh peeng-chee) 开瓶器 | |
| boulevard | *dadao* (dah-dow) 大道 | |

| | | |
|---|---|---|
| bowl | *wan* (wahn) | 碗 |
| box | *hezi* (her-dzu) | 盒子 |
| boxing | *quanji* (chwahn-jee) | 拳击 |
| boy | *nanhair* (nahn-high-urr) | 男孩 |
| boyfriend | *nan pengyou* (nahn perng-you) | 男朋友 |
| bra | *ruzhao* (roo-jow) | 乳罩 |
| branch office | *fen bu* (fern boo) | 分部 |
| brand | *shangbiao* (shahng-bee-ow) | 商标 |
| bread | *mianbao* (mee-an-bow) | 面包 |
| breast | *rufang* (roo-fahng) | 乳房 |
| bride | *xinniang* (sheen-nee-ahng) | 新娘 |
| bridegroom | *xinlang* (sheen-lahng) | 新郎 |
| bridge | *qiao* (chow) | 桥 |
| brother | *xiongdi* (she-ong-dee) | 兄弟 |
| Buddhism | *Fojiao* (Fwo-jow) | 佛教 |
| Buddhist | *Fojiaotu* (Fwo-jow too) | 佛教徒 |
| budget | *yusuan* (yuuswahn) | 预算 |
| buffet | *zizhucan* (dzu-joo-tsahn) | 自助餐 |
| buffet dinner | *zizhu wancan* (dzu-joo wahn-tsahn) 自助晚餐 | |
| buffet lunch | *zizhu wucan* (dzu-joo woo-tsahn) 自助午餐 | |
| building | *loufang* (low-fahng) | 楼房 |
| businessperson | *shangren* (shahng-wren) | 商人 |
| busy | *mang* (mahng) | 忙 |
| butter | *huangyou* (hwahng-yoe) | 黄油 |

**[C]**

| | | |
|---|---|---|
| cabbage | *kongxin cai* (kohng sheen tsigh) | 空心菜 |
| cabin | *kecang* (ker-tsahng) | 客仓 |
| cable television | *bilu dianshi* (bee-loo dee-an-shr) 闭路电视 | |
| café | *kafeiguan* (kah-fay-gwahn) | 咖啡馆 |
| cafeteria | *shitang* (shr-tahng) | 食堂 |

| | | |
|---|---|---|
| calculator | *jisuanji* (jee-swahn-jee) | 计算机 |
| canal | *yunhe* (ywun-her) | 运河 |
| cancel | *quxiao* (chwee-she-ow) | 撤消 |
| capital (city) | *shoudu* (show-doo) | 首都 |
| cash | *xianjin* (shee-an-jeen) | 现金 |
| cashier | *caiwu* (tsigh-woo) | 财务 |
| casual | *suibian* (sway-bee-an) | 随便 |
| centigrade | *sheshi* (sher-shr) | 摄氏 |
| central | *zhongyang* (johng-yahng) | 中央 |
| cereal | *maipian* (my-pee-an) | 麦片 |
| ceremony | *dianli* (dee-an-lee) | 典礼 |
| chair | *yizi* (ee-dzu) | 椅子 |
| change (money) | *lingqian* (leeng-chee-an) | 零钱 |
| changing money | *duihuan* (dway-hwahn) | 兑换 |
| cheap | *pianyi* (pee-an-ee) | 便宜 |
| check | *zhipiao* (jr-pee-ow) | 支票 |
| check in (at airport) | *ban cheng shouxu* (bahn cherng show-shee) | 办程手续 |
| check out (hotel) | *tuifang* (tway-fahng) | 退房 |
| cheongsam (dress) | *qipao* (chee-pow) | 旗袍 |
| child | *haizi* (high-dzu) | 孩子 |
| chocolate | *qiaokeli* (chiao-ker-lee) | 巧克力 |
| chopsticks | *kuaizi* (kwie-dzu) | 筷子 |
| church | *jiaotang* (jow-tahng) | 教堂 |
| city, town | *chengshi* (cherng-shr) | 城市 |
| city map | *chengshi jiaotong tu* (cherng-shr jow-tohng too) | 城市交通图 |
| classmate | *tongxue* (tohng-shway) | 同学 |
| cloakroom | *yimaojian* (ee-mao-jee-an) | 衣帽间 |
| closing time | *guan men* (gwahn mern) | 关门 |
| clothing | *yifu* (ee-foo) | 衣服 |
| club (recreational) | *julebu* (jwee-ler-boo) | 俱乐部 |
| coach, bus | *changtuqiche* (chahng-too-chee-cher) | 长途汽车 |

| | |
|---|---|
| coat | *dayi* (dah-ee) 大衣 |
| cocktail | *jiweijiu* (jee-way-jew) 鸡尾酒 |
| cocktail party | *jiweijiuhui* (jee-way-jew-hway) 鸡尾酒会 |
| cold dishes (appetizers) | *lengpan* (lerng-pahn) 冷盘 |
| color | *yanse* (yahn-suh) 颜色 |
| comedy | *xiju* (see-jwee) 戏剧 |
| comfortable | *shufu* (shoo-foo) 舒服 |
| Communist party | *Gongchangdang* (Gohng-chahng-dahng) 共产党 |
| concert | *yinyuehui* (een-yway-hway) 音乐会 |
| condom | *biyun tao* (bee-yuun-tao) 避孕套 |
| Confucius | *Kongzi* (Koong-dzu) 孔子 |
| congratulations | *gongxi* (gohng-see) 恭喜 |
| contact lenses | *yinxing yanjing* (yeen-sheeng yahn-jeeng) 隐形眼镜 |
| corner (street) | *guaijiao* (gwie-jow) 拐角 |
| correct | *dui* (dway) 对 |
| counter (sales) | *guitai* (gway-tie) 柜台 |
| counter (service) | *fuwutai* (foo-woo-tie) 服务台 |
| country (nation) | *guojia* (gwoh-jah) 国家 |
| countryside | *noncun* (nohng-tswun) 农村 |
| cream | *naiyou* (nigh-you) 奶油 |
| crowd | *renqun* (wren-chween) 人群 |
| crowded | *yongji* (yohng-jee) 拥挤 |
| cultural | *wenhua* (wern-hwah) 文化 |
| cultural exchange | *wenhua jiaoliu* (wern-hwah jee-ow lew) 文化交流 |
| culture | *wenhua* (wern-hwah) 文化 |
| currency | *huobi* (hwoh-bee) 货币 |
| custom (way) | *fengsu* (foong-soo) 风俗 |
| customer | *guke* (goo-ker) 顾客 |
| Customs | *Haiguan* (High-gwahn) 海关 |
| Customs tariff | *Guanshui* (Gwahn-shway) 关税 |

**[D]**

| | | |
|---|---|---|
| dad | *baba* (bah-bah) | 爸爸 |
| daily | *meitian* (may-tee-an) | 每天 |
| daily paper | *ri bao* (rr bow) | 日报 |
| dance (verb) | *tiaowu* (tee-ow-woo) | 跳舞 |
| dance hall | *wu ting* (woo teeng) | 舞厅 |
| dance party | *wu hui* (woo hway) | 舞会 |
| date (courting) | *yuehui* (yway-hway) | 约会 |
| degree (college) | *xuewei* (shway-way) | 学位 |
| delicatessen | *shushi dian* (shoo-shr dee-an) | 熟食店 |
| democracy | *minzhu* (meen-joo) | 民主 |
| demonstration | *shiwei* (shr-way) | 示威 |
| department | *bu* (boo) | 部 |
| departure | *chufa* (chwee-fah) | 出发 |
| deposit (money) | *yajin* (yah-jeen) | 押金 |
| dessert | *tianpin* (tee-an-peen) | 甜品 |
| dictionary | *zidian* (dzu-dee-an) | 字典 |
| diplomat | *waijiaojia* (weigh-jee-ow-jah) | 外交家 |
| disabled person | *canfei renshi* (tsahn-fay-wren-shr) 残废人士 | |
| disco | *di si ge ting* (dee-ss-ger teeng) | 迪斯歌厅 |
| discount | *zhekou* (juh-koe) | 折扣 |
| divorce | *lihun* (lee-hwun) | 离婚 |
| domestic | *guonei* (gwoh-nay) | 国内 |
| dormitory | *sushe* (soo-sher) | 宿舍 |
| downtown | *shizhongxin* (shr-johng-sheen) | 市中心 |
| Dragon Boat Festival | *Duan Wu Jie* (Dwahn Woo Jeh) | 端午节 |
| dragon boat race | *long zhou bisai* (lohng joe bee-sigh) 龙舟比赛 | |
| dress (noun) | *yifu* (ee-foo) | 衣服 |
| drinking straw | *xiguan* (she-gwahn) | 吸管 |
| driver | *siji* (suh-jee) | 司机 |
| driver's license | *jiashi zhizhao* (jah-shr jr-chow) 驾驶执照 | |

| | |
|---|---|
| drugstore | *yaodian* (yow-dee-an) 药店 |
| drunk, tipsy | *zui* (zway) 醉 |
| duck | *ya* (yah) 鸭 |
| dust | *huichen* (hway-chern) 灰尘 |
| duty (customs) | *shui* (shway) 税 |
| duty free | *mianshui* (mee-an-shway) 免税 |

**[E]**

| | |
|---|---|
| early | *zao* (zow) 早 |
| earphone | *erji* (urr-jee) 耳机 |
| earthquake | *dizhen* (dee-jun) 地震 |
| east | *dong* (dohng) 东 |
| East China Sea | *Dong Hai* (Dohng High) 东海 |
| economy | *jingji* (jeeng-jee) 经济 |
| editor | *bianji* (bee-an-jee) 编辑 |
| election | *xuanju* (shwen-jwee) 选举 |
| electric plug | *dian chatou* (dee-an chah-toe) 电插头 |
| elevator | *dianti* (dee-an-tee) 电梯 |
| emergency room | *jizhen shi* (jee-jun shr) 急诊室 |
| English language | *Yingwen* (Eeng-wern) 英文 |
| entrance | *rukou* (roo-koe) 入口 |
| entry visa | *rujing qianzheng* (roo-jeeng chee-an-zhehng) 入境签证 |
| error | *cuowu* (tswoh-woo) 错误 |
| escalator | *zidongfuti* (dzu-dohng-foo-tee) 自动扶梯 |
| Europe | *Ouzhou* (Oh-joe) 欧洲 |
| European (person) | *Ouzhouren* (Oh-joe-wren) 欧洲人 |
| evening | *wanshang* (wahn-shahng) 晚上 |
| evening dress | *wan lifu* (wahn lee-foo) 晚礼服 |
| evening party | *wan hui* (wahn hway) 晚会 |
| exhausted | *leihuai-le* (lay-hwie-luh) 累坏了 |
| exhibition | *zhanlanhui* (jahn-lahn-hway) 展览会 |
| exhibition hall | *zhanlan guan* (jahn-lahn gwahn) 展览馆 |
| exit | *chukou* (choo-koe) 出口 |
| expenses | *feiyong* (fay-yohng) 费用 |

| | | |
|---|---|---|
| expensive | *gui* (gway) 贵 | |
| expert | *shulian* (shuu-lee-an) 熟练 | |
| extension cord | *jiechang dianxian* (jeh-chang dee-an-she-an) 结肠电线 | |
| eyedrops | *yanyaoshui* (yahn-yow-shway) 眼药水 | |
| eyeglasses | *yanjing* (yahn-jeeng) 眼镜 | |

**[F]**

| | |
|---|---|
| face | *lian* (lee-an) 脸 |
| factory | *gongchang* (gohng-chahng) 工厂 |
| Fahrenheit | *Huashi* (hwah-shr) 华氏 |
| faint | *touyun* (toe-ywun) 头昏 |
| fake | *maopai* (mao-pie) 冒牌 |
| fall (verb) | *shuaidao* (shoo-ai-dow) 摔倒 |
| family | *jia* (jah) 家 |
| family members | *qin ren* (cheen wren) 亲人 |
| famous | *youming* (you-meeng) 有名 |
| famous dish | *ming cai* (meeng tsigh) 名菜 |
| far | *yuan* (ywahn) 远 |
| farm | *nongchang* (nohng-chahng) 农场 |
| farmer | *nongfu* (nohng-foo) 农夫 |
| fast food | *kuai can* (kwie tsahn) 快餐 |
| fashion | *shimao* (shr-mao) 时髦 |
| fault | *cuo* (tswoh) 错 |
| fee, expense | *feiyong* (fay-yohng) 费用 |
| female | *nu* (nwee) 女 |
| festival | *jieri* (jeer-rr) 节日 |
| fiancé | *weihunfu* (way-hwun-foo) 未婚夫 |
| fine, penalty | *fakuan* (fah-kwahn) 罚款 |
| fire (conflagration) | *huozai* (hwoh-zigh) 火灾 |
| fire alarm | *huo jing* (hwoh jeeng) 火警 |
| fire escape | *anquan ti* (ahn-chwahn tee) 安全梯 |
| fire exit | *taiping men* (tie-peeng mern) 太平门 |
| firecracker | *bianpao* (bee-an pow) 鞭炮 |
| first-aid kit | *ji jiu xiang* (jee jeo she-ahng) 急救箱 |

| | | |
|---|---|---|
| first-class | *tou-deng* (toe-derng) | 头等 |
| fish | *yu* (yuu) | 鱼 |
| flag | *qizi* (chee-dzu) | 旗子 |
| flashlight | *shoudiantong* (show-dee-an-toong) 手电筒 | |
| flood | *shuizai* (shway-zigh) | 水灾 |
| flowers | *hua* (hwah-urr) | 花儿 |
| flower shop | *hua dian* (hwah dee-an) | 花店 |
| folk dance | *minjian wudao* (meen-jee-an woo-dow) 民间舞蹈 | |
| folk music | *minjian yinyue* (meen-jee-an een-yway) 民间音乐 | |
| food poisoning | *shiwu zhongdu* (shr-woo johng-doo) 食物中毒 | |
| foreign | *waiguo-de* (wigh-gwoh-der) 外国的 | |
| foreign exchange | *waihui* (wigh-hway) 外汇 | |
| foreign guest | *wai bin* (wigh been) 外宾 | |
| forest | *shulin* (shoo-leen) 树林 | |
| free (cost) | *mianfei* (mee-an-fay) 免费 | |
| free (time) | *you kong* (you kohng) 有空 | |
| free trade zone | *ziyou maoyiqu* (dzu-you mao-ee-choo) 自由贸易 | |
| freezing | *bingdong* (beeng-doong) 冰冻 | |
| frozen food | *lengcang shipin* (lerng-tsahng shr-peen) 冷藏食品 | |
| fruit | *shuiguo* (shway-gwoh) 水果 | |
| fruit juice | *guozhi* (gwoh-jr) 果汁 | |
| fruit store | *shuiguo dian* (shway-gwoh dee-an) 水果店 | |
| full | *man-le* (mahn-ler) 满了 | |
| full stomach | *bao* (bow) 饱 | |
| fuse (noun) | *baoxiansi* (bow-shee-an-suh) 保险丝 | |
| | | |
| **[G]** | | |
| gamble | *dubuo* (doo-bwoh) 赌博 | |

110

| | | |
|---|---|---|
| gambling house | *du chang* (doo chahng) | 赌场 |
| game, match | *qiusai* (cheo-sigh) | 球赛 |
| garbage | *laji* (lah-jee) | 垃圾 |
| garden | *huayuan* (hwah-ywahn) | 花园 |
| garlic | *suan* (swahn) | 蒜 |
| gasoline | *qiyou* (chee-you) | 汽油 |
| gasoline station | *jiayou zhan* (jah-you jahn) | 加油站 |
| German | *Dewen* (Duh-wern) | 德文 |
| ginseng | *renshen* (wren-shern) | 人参 |
| girl | *nuhaizi* (nwee-high-dzu) | 女孩子 |
| girlfriend | *nupengyou* (nwee-perng-you) | 女朋友 |
| glasses (eye) | *yanjing* (yahn-jeeng) | 眼镜 |
| gloves | *shoutao* (show-tou) | 手套 |
| gold | *jin* (jeen) | 金 |
| goldfish | *jin yu* (jeen yuu) | 金鱼 |
| golf | *gaoerfuqiu* (gow-urr-foo-cheo) | 高尔夫球 |
| goose | *e* (er) | 鹅 |
| government office | *ji guan* (jee gwahn) | 机官 |
| gram | *ke* (ker) | 克 |
| grandfather | *zufu* (zoo-foo) | 祖父 |
| grandmother | *zumu* (zoo-moo) | 祖母 |
| grandparents | *zufumu* (zoo-foo-moo) | 祖父母 |
| grapes | *putao* (poo-taow) | 葡萄 |
| grass | *cao* (tsaow) | 草 |
| great, big | *da* (dah) | 大 |
| guest | *keren* (ker-wren) | 客人 |
| guest house | *bin guan* (been gwahn) | 宾馆 |
| guide | *daoyou* (dow-you) | 导游 |
| guidebook | *luyou zhinan* (lwee-you jr-nahn) | 旅游指南 |
| gym | *tiyuguan* (tee-yuu-gwahn) | 体育馆 |
| gymnastics | *ticao* (tee-tsow) | 体操 |
| gynecologist | *fukeyisheng* (foo-ker-ee-sherng) | 妇科医生 |

**[H]**

| | |
|---|---|
| **half** | *ban* (bahn) 半 |
| **hall (meeting)** | *guan* (gwahn) 馆 |
| **handbag** | *shoutibao* (show-tee-bow) 手提包 |
| **handball** | *shouqiu* (show-cheo) 手球 |
| **handicapped person** | *canji ren shi* (tsahn-jee wren shr) 残疾人士 |
| **handicraft** | *shougongyi pin* (show-gohng-ee-peen) 手工艺品 |
| **Happy Birthday** | *shengri kuaile* (sherng rr kwai ler) 生日快乐 |
| **harvest** | *shouhou* (show-hoe) 收获 |
| **hay fever** | *kucao re* (koo tsow ruh) 枯草热 |
| **health club** | *jianshen fang* (jee-an-shern fahng) 健身房 |
| **heart attack** | *xinzangbing fazuo* (sheen-zahng-beeng fah-zwoh) 心脏病发作 |
| **high school** | *zhong xue* (johng shway) 中学 |
| **highway** | *gonglu* (gohng-loo) 公路 |
| **hill** | *xiaoshan* (shou-shahn) 小山 |
| **history** | *lishi* (lee-shr) 历史 |
| **holiday** | *jiaqi* (jah-chee) 假期 |
| **home** | *jia* (jah) 家 |
| **hometown** | *guxiang* (goo-she-ahng) 故乡 |
| | *jiaxiang* (jah-she-ahng) 家乡 |
| **homosexual** | *tongxinglian* (tohng-sheeng-lee-an) 同性恋 |
| **honey** | *fengmi* (ferng-mee) 蜂蜜 |
| **Hong Kong** | *Xiang Gang* (Shee-ahng Gahng) 香港 |
| **house** | *fangwu* (fahng-woo) 房屋 |
| **housewife** | *funu* (foo-nwee) 妇女 |
| **hurry** | *henji* (hern-jee) 很急 |
| **husband** | *zhangfu* (jahng-foo) 丈夫 |

**[I]**

| | |
|---|---|
| **ice** | *bing* (beeng) 冰 |

112

| ice cream | *bing qilin* (beeng chee-leen) 冰淇淋 |
| ice skating | *hua bing* (hwah beeng) 滑冰 |
| ice water | *bing shui* (been shway) 冰水 |
| illegal | *buhefa* (boo-her-fah) 不和法 |
| important | *zhongyao* (johng-yee-ow) 重要 |
| impossible | *bukeneng* (boo-ker-nerng) 不可能 |
| industry | *gongye* (gohng-yeh) 工业 |
| inexpensive | *pianyi* (pee-an-ee) 便宜 |
| informal | *feizhenshi* (fay-jern-shr) 非正式 |
| information (news) | *xiaoxi* (she-ow-she) 消息 |
| information desk | *wenxunchu* (wern-shwun-choo) 问讯处 |
| injection | *zhushe* (joo-sher) 注射 |
| insurance | *baoxian* (bow-shee-an) 保险 |
| interesting | *youyisi* (you-ee-suh) 有意思 |
| intermission | *mujian xiuxi* (moo-jee-an she-oh-she) 幕间休息 |
| international | *guoji* (gwoh-jee) 国际 |
| interpreter | *fanyi* (fahn-ee) 翻译 |
| intersection (streets) | *shizilukou* (shr-dzu-loo-koe) 十字路口 |
| invitation | *qingtie* (cheeng-tee-eh) 请帖 |
| ivory | *xiangya* (shee-ahng-yah) 象牙 |

[J]
| jacket | *duanshangyi* (dwahn-shahng-ee) 短上衣 |
| jade | *yu* (yuu) 玉 |
| jail, prison | *jianyu* (jee-an-yuu) 监狱 |
| jeans | *niuzaiku* (new-zigh-koo) 牛仔裤 |
| jewelry | *zhubao* (joo-bow) 珠宝 |
| joke (noun) | *xiaohua* (she-ow-hwah) 笑话 |
| journalist | *jizhe* (jee-juh) 记者 |
| journey | *luxing* (lwee-sheeng) 旅行 |
| juice (fruit) | *guozhi* (gwoh-jr) 果汁 |
| jumper/sweater | *maoyi* (mao-ee) 毛衣 |
| jungle | *conglin* (tsohng-leen) 丛林 |
| justice | *gongzheng* (gohng-jerng) 公正 |

**[K]**

| | |
|---|---|
| key | *yaoshi* (yow-shr) 钥匙 |
| kilogram | *gongjin* (gohng-jeen) 公斤 |
| kilometer | *gongli* (gohng-lee) 公里 |
| kindergarten | *youeryuan* (you-urr-ywahn) 幼儿园 |
| kiss | *wen* (wern) 吻 |
| kitchen | *chufang* (choo-fahng) 厨房 |
| kite | *fengzheng* (ferng-jerng) 风筝 |
| kleenex | *zhijin* (jr-jeen) 纸巾 |
| Korea | *Chaoxian* (Chow-she-an) 朝鲜 |
| Kyoto | *Jingdu* (Jeeng-doo) 京都 |

**[L]**

| | |
|---|---|
| lacquerware | *qiqi* (chee-chee) 漆器 |
| lake | *hu* (hoo) 湖 |
| lamb (meat) | *yangrou* (yahng-row) 羊肉 |
| landlord | *fangzhu* (fahng-joo) 房主 |
| language | *yuyan* (yuu-yahn) 语言 |
| late | *wan* (wahn) 晚 |
| law | *falu* (fah-lwee) 法律 |
| lawyer | *lushi* (lwee-shr) 律师 |
| leader | *lingdao* (leeng-dow) 领导 |
| leave (depart) | *likai* (lee-kigh) 离开 |
| leave a message | *liu hua* (leo hwah) 留话 |
| lecture | *jiangyan* (jee-ahng-yahn) 讲演 |
| leisure time | *kongxian shijian* (kohng-shee-an shr-jee-an) 空闲时间 |
| letter | *xin* (sheen) 信 |
| library | *tushuguan* (too-shoo-gwahn) 图书馆 |
| license | *zuce zheng* (joo-tser-zherng) 注册证 |
| liquor | *baijiu* (by-jeo) 白酒 |
| literature | *wenxue* (wern-shway) 文学 |
| lock | *suo* (swoh) 锁 |
| longevity | *changshou* (chahng-show) 长寿 |

| | |
|---|---|
| **Los Angeles** | *Luo Shanji* (Lwoh Shahn-jee) 洛杉矶 |
| **lost-and-found** | *shiwu zhaoling* (shr-woo jow-leeng) 失物招领 |
| **love (verb)** | *ai* (aye) 爱 |
| **luck** | *yunqi* (ywun-chee) 运气 |
| **luggage** | *xingli* (sheeng-lee) 行李 |
| **lunar calendar** | *yin li* (een lee) 阴历 |

**[M]**

| | |
|---|---|
| **Macao** | *Aomen* (Ow-mern) 澳门 |
| **magzine** | *zazhi* (zah-jr) 杂志 |
| **magic** | *moshu* (mwo-shoo) 魔术 |
| **mahjong** | *majiang* (mah-jee-ahng) 麻将 |
| **mainland** | *dalu* (dah-loo) 大陆 |
| **main station** | *zong zhan* (zohng jahn) 终站 |
| **male** | *nan* (nahn) 男 |
| **man, male** | *nanren* (nahn-wren) 男人 |
| **management** | *guanli* (gwahn-lee) 管理 |
| **manager** | *jingli* (jeeng-lee) 经理 |
| **massage** | *anmo* (ahn-mwo) 按摩 |
| **mechanic** | *jigong* (jee-gohng) 技工 |
| **message** | *liuhua* (leo-hwah) 留话 |
| **military** | *junshi* (jwin-shr) 军事 |
| **milk** | *niunai* (new-nigh) 牛奶 |
| **miniskirt** | *chao duanqun* (chow dwahn-chwun) 超短裙 |
| **model (fashion)** | *moter* (mwo-ter-urr) 模特儿 |
| **monosodium glutamate** | *weijing* (way-jeeng) 味精 |
| **Moscow** | *Mosike* (Mwo-suh-ker) 莫斯科 |
| **mountain** | *shan* (shahn) 山 |
| **movie** | *dianying* (dee-an eeng) 电影 |
| **movie theater** | *dianying yuan* (dee-an-eeng ywahn) 电影院 |

| | | |
|---|---|---|
| museum | *bowuguan* (bwo-woo-gwahn) | 博物馆 |
| music | *yinyue* (een-yway) | 音乐 |
| Muslim | *Huijiaotu* (Hway-jee-ow-too) | 回教徒 |

**[N]**

| | | |
|---|---|---|
| nap | *xiaoshui* (shiaow-shway) | 小睡 |
| nation | *guo* (gwoh) | 国 |
| national | *guojia* (gwoh-jah) | 国家 |
| nationality | *guoji* (gwoh-jee) | 国籍 |
| native dress | *guo fu* (gwoh-foo) | 国服 |
| neighbor | *linju* (leen-jwee) | 邻居 |
| new | *xin* (sheen) | 新 |
| news | *xinwen* (sheen-wern) | 新闻 |
| newspaper | *baozhi* (bow-jr) | 报纸 |
| New Year | *Xin Nian* (Sheen Nee-an) | 新年 |
| New Year's Eve | *Chu Xi* (Chwoo She) | 除夕 |
| nightclub | *ye zonghui* (Yeh johng-hway) | 夜总会 |
| north | *bei* (bay) | 北 |
| North America | *Bei Meizhou* (Bay May-joe) | 北美洲 |
| nuclear | *he* (her) | 赫 |
| nurse | *hushi* (hoo-shr) | 护士 |
| nursery | *tuoersuo* (twoh-urr-swoh) | 托儿所 |

**[O]**

| | | |
|---|---|---|
| oatmeal | *maipian* (my-pee-an) | 麦片 |
| occupation | *zhiye* (jr-yeh) | 职业 |
| ocean | *haiyang* (high-yahng) | 海洋 |
| office | *bangongshi* (bahn-gohng-shr) | 办公室 |
| official (bureaucrat) | *guan* (gwahn) | 官 |
| old (person) | *lao* (lao) | 老 |
| one-way | *dan-cheng* (dahn-cherng) | 单程 |
| open | *kaimen* (kigh-mern) | 开门 |
| opera | *geju* (ger-jwee) | 歌剧 |
| orange juice | *juzi zhi* (jwee-dzu jr) | 橘子汁 |
| outlet (electric) | *chazuo* (chah-zwoh) | 插座 |

| | |
|---|---|
| overcoat | *dayi* (dah-ee) 大衣 |
| overseas | *guowai* (gwoh-wigh) 国外 |
| Overseas Chinese | *Hua Qiao* (Hwah Chee-ow) 华侨 |
| owner | *suoyouren* (swoh-you-wren) 所有人 |

**[P]**

| | |
|---|---|
| Pacific Ocean | *Taiping Yang* (Tie-peeng Yahng) 太平洋 |
| package | *baoguo* (bow-gwoh) 包裹 |
| pagoda | *baota* (bow-tah) 宝塔 |
| palace | *gongdian* (gohng-dee-an) 宫殿 |
| panda bear | *xiong mao* (shee-ong mao) 熊猫 |
| Paris | *Bali* (Bah-lee) 巴黎 |
| parking lot | *tingche chang* (teeng-cher chahng) 停车场 |
| party (recreational) | *juhui* (jwee-hway) 聚会 |
| passenger | *luke* (lwee-ker) 旅客 |
| passport | *huzhao* (hoo-jow) 护照 |
| passport number | *huzhao haoma* (hoo-jow how-mah) 护照号码 |
| pastry | *gaodian* (gow-dee-an) 糕点 |
| peace | *heping* (her-peeng) 和平 |
| peanuts | *huasheng* (hwah-sherng) 花生 |
| Pearl River | *Zhu Jiang* (Joo Jee-ahang) 珠江 |
| pearls | *zhenzhu* (zhern-joo) 珍珠 |
| Peking Duck | *Beijing Kaoya* (Bay-jeeng kow-yah) 北京烤鸭 |
| penicillin | *qingmeisu* (cheeng-may-soo) 青霉素 |
| performance | *yanchu* (yahn-choo) 演出 |
| performer | *yanyuan* (yahn-ywahn) 演员 |
| permission | *xuke* (she-ker) 许可 |
| pharmacy | *yaodian* (yow-dee-an) 药店 |
| physical exam | *ti jian* (tee jee-an) 体检 |
| pingpong | *pingpangqiu* (peeng-pahng-cheo) 乒乓球 |
| platform (train) | *zhantai* (jahn-tie) 站台 |

| | |
|---|---|
| play (theatrical) | *xiju* (she-jwee) 戏剧 |
| playground | *caochang* (tsow-chahng) 操场 |
| police station | *gongan ju* (gohng-ahn jwee) 公安局 |
| pollution | *wuran* (woo-rahn) 污染 |
| population | *renkou* (wren-koe) 人口 |
| pottery | *taoqi* (tou-chee) 陶器 |
| premier | *zongli* (zohng-lee) 总理 |
| prescription | *yaofang* (yee-ow-fahng) 药方 |
| president<br>  (company) | *zongcai* (zohng-tsigh) 总裁 |
| president (country) | *zongtong* (zohng-tohng) 总统 |
| printed matter | *yinshua pin* (een-shwah peen) 印刷品 |
| prison | *jianyu* (jee-an-yuu) 监狱 |
| profession | *zhiye* (jr-yeh) 职业 |
| prostitute | *jinu* (jee-nwee) 妓女 |
| province | *sheng* (sherng) 省 |
| public | *gonggong* (gohng-gohng) 公共 |
| public square | *guang chang* (gwahng chahng) 广场 |
| purse, handbag | *shoutibao* (show-tee-bow) 手提包 |

**[Q]**

| | |
|---|---|
| quality | *zhiliang* (jr-lee-ahng) 质量 |
| quantity | *shuliang* (shoo-lee-ahng) 数量 |
| question | *wenti* (wern-tee) 问题 |
| queue | *paidui* (pie-dway) 排队 |
| quick, fast | *kuai* (kwie) 快 |
| quiet, peaceful | *anjing* (ahn-jeeng) 安静 |

**[R]**

| | |
|---|---|
| race (human) | *zhongzu* (johng-joo) 种族 |
| racism | *zhongzupianjian* (johng-joo-pee-an-jee-an) 种族偏见 |
| raincoat | *yuyi* (yuu-ee) 雨衣 |
| rape | *qiangjian* (chee-ahng-jee-an) 强奸 |

118

| | |
|---|---|
| receipt | *shouju* (show-jwee) 收据 |
| reception, party | *zhaodaihui* (jow-die-hway) 招待会 |
| refund | *tuikuan* (tway-kwahn) 推款 |
| region | *diqu* (dee-chwee) 地区 |
| relative, kin | *qinqi* (cheen-chee) 亲戚 |
| repair | *xiu* (shew) 修 |
| resident permit | *juliu zheng* (jwee-leo zherng) 居留证 |
| rest | *xiuxi* (shew-she) 休息 |
| reverse charges | *duifangfufei* (dway-fahng-foo-fay) 对方付费 |
| rice (cooked) | *baifan* (by-fahn) 白饭 |
| rich | *fuyou* (foo-you) 富有 |
| ring (jewelry) | *jiezhi* (jeh-jr) 戒指 |
| river | *he* (her) 河 |
| road | *lu* (loo) 路 |
| room number | *fangjian haoma* (fahng-jee-an how-mah) 房间号码 |
| round-trip | *laihui* (lie-hway) 来回 |
| round-trip ticket | *laihui piao* (lie-hway pee-ow) 来回票 |
| row, line, queue | *pai* (pie) 排 |
| ruins | *feixu* (fay-shee) 废墟 |

**[S]**

| | |
|---|---|
| safe (adjective) | *anquan* (ahn-chwahn) 安全 |
| safe (noun) | *baoxianxiang* (bow-she-an-she-ahng) 保险箱 |
| sales tax | *yingye shui* (eeng-yeh shway) 营业税 |
| sandwich | *sanmingzhi* (sahn-meeng-jr) 三明治 |
| San Francisco | *Jiujin Shan* (Jeo-jeen Shahn) 旧金山 |
| satellite | *weixing* (way-sheeng) 卫星 |
| scenery | *fengjing* (ferng-jeeng) 风景 |
| school | *xuexiao* (shway-she-ow) 学校 |
| scientist | *kexuejia* (ker-shway-jah) 科学家 |
| seafood | *haixian* (high-she-an) 海鲜 |

| | | |
|---|---|---|
| secretary | *mishu* (me-shoo) 秘书 | |
| security guard | *anquan renyuan* (ahn-chwahn wren-ywahn) 安全人员 | |
| seminar | *yantaohui* (yahn-tow-hway) 研讨会 | |
| Seoul | *Hancheng* (Hahn-chweeng) 汉城 | |
| service fee | *fuwu fei* (foo-woo fay) 服务费 | |
| sex | *xing* (sheeng) 性 | |
| ship | *chuan* (chwahn) 船 | |
| shopping area | *shangyequ* (shahng-yeh-chwee) 商业区 | |
| Siberia | *Xiboliya* (She-bwo-lee-yah) 西伯利亚 | |
| signature | *qianming* (chee-an meeng) 签名 | |
| Silk Road | *Sichou Zhi Lu* (Suh-choe Jr Loo) 丝绸之路 | |
| sleep | *shuijiao* (shway-jee-ow) 睡觉 | |
| society | *shehui* (sher-hway) 社会 | |
| soda water | *qi shui* (chee shway) 汽水 | |
| soft drink | *qingliang yinliao* (cheeng-lee-ahng een-lee-ow) 清凉饮料 | |
| soldier | *zhanshi* (jahn-shr) 战士 | |
| south | *nan* (nahn) 南 | |
| South China Sea | *Nan Hai* (Nahn High) 南海 | |
| souvenir | *jinianpin* (jee-nee-an-peen) 纪念品 | |
| souvenir shop | *jinianpin dian* (jee-nee-an-peen dee-an) 纪念品店 | |
| space shuttle | *hangtian feiji* (hahng-tee-an fay-jee) 航天飞机 | |
| sports | *yundong* (yuun-dohng) 运动 | |
| stadium | *tiyuchang* (tee-yuu-chahng) 体育场 | |
| study | *shufang* (shoo-fahng) 书房 | |
| study abroad | *liuxue* (lew-shway) 留学 | |
| suit (western wear) | *xifu* (she-foo) 西服 | |
| sunglasses | *mojing* (mo-jeeng) 墨镜 | |
| Sun Yatsen | *Sun Zhongshan* (Soon Johng-shahn) 孙中山 | |

| | | |
|---|---|---|
| swimming pool | *youyong chi* (you-yohng chr) 游泳池 | |
| symphony | *jiaoxiangyue* (jow-she-ahng-yway) 交响乐 | |

**[T]**

| | |
|---|---|
| table tennis | *pingpangqiu* (peeng-pahng-cheo) 乒乓球 |
| taste, flavor | *wei* (way) 味 |
| tax free | *mian shui* (mee-an shway) 免税 |
| teacher | *jiaoshi* (jow-shr) 教师 |
| teahouse | *chaguan* (chah-gwahn) 茶馆 |
| technology transfer | *jishu zhuanrang* (jee-shoo jwahn-rahng) 技术转让 |
| television | *dianshi* (dee-an-shr) 电视 |
| temple | *siyuan* (suh-ywahn) 寺院 |
| Thailand | *Taiguo* (Tie-gwoh) 泰国 |
| theater | *juchang* (jwee-chahng) 剧场 |
| theater tickets | *xipiao* (she-pee-ow) 戏票 |
| Tibet | *Xizang* (She-zahng) 西藏 |
| tiger | *laohu* (lao-hoo) 老虎 |
| tip (gratuity) | *xiaofei* (shiaow-fay) 小费 |
| toilet paper | *ce zhi* (tzer jr) 厕纸 |
| Tokyo | *Dongjing* (Dohng-jeeng) 东京 |
| tour | *luxing* (lwee-sheeng) 旅行 |
| tour escort | *lingdui* (leeng-dway) 领队 |
| tour group | *luxingtuan* (lwee-sheeng-twahn) 旅行团 |
| tourist | *luke* (lwee-kuh) 旅客 |
| tournament | *bisai* (bee-sigh) 比赛 |
| trade fair | *jiaoyi hui* (jow-ee hway) 交易会 |
| trademark | *shang biao* (shahg bee-ow) 商标 |
| translate, translator | *fanyi* (fahn-ee) 翻译，翻译员 |
| transportation | *yunshu* (ywun-shoo) 运输 |
| transportation charges | *yunshu feiyong* (ywun-shoo fay-yohng) 运输费用 |
| tutor | *daoshi* (dow-shr) 导师 |

| | | |
|---|---|---|
| **typewriter** | *daziji* (dah-dzu-jee) | 打字机 |
| **typhoon** | *taifeng* (tie-ferng) | 台风 |
| **typist** | *daziyuan* (dah-dzu-ywahn) | 打字员 |

**[U]**

| | | |
|---|---|---|
| **umbrella** | *yusan* (yuu-sahn) | 雨伞 |
| **unacceptable** | *buxing* (boo-sheeng) | 不行 |
| **uncle** | *bofu* (bwo-foo) | 伯父 |
| **uncomfortable** | *bushufu* (boo-shoo-foo) | 不舒服 |
| **uniform** | *zhifu* (jr-foo) | 制服 |
| **United Nations** | *Lianhe Guo* (Lee-an-her Gwoh) | 联合国 |
| **United States** | *Meiguo* (May-gwoh) | 美国 |
| **universe** | *yuzhou* (yuu-joe) | 宇宙 |
| **urinate** | *xiaobian* (shiaow-bee-an) | 小便 |

**[V]**

| | | |
|---|---|---|
| **vacancy** | *kongfang* (kohng-fahng) | 空房 |
| **vacation** | *fangjia* (fahng-jah) | 放假 |
| **vegetarian** | *sushi* (soo-shr) | 素食 |
| **venereal disease** | *xingbing* (sheeng-beeng) | 性病 |
| **Vietnam** | *Yuenan* (Yway-nahn) | 越南 |
| **village** | *cunzhuang* (tswun-jwahng) | 村庄 |
| **volleyball** | *paiqiu* (pie-cheo) | 排球 |
| **vomit** | *outu* (oh-too) | 呕吐 |

**[W]**

| | | |
|---|---|---|
| **wage, salary** | *gongzi* (gohng-dzu) | 工资 |
| **waiting room** | *houche shi* (hoe-cher shr) | 候车室 |
| **wallet** | *pijiazi* (pee-jah-dzu) | 皮夹子 |
| **wall poster** | *qiang bao* (cheen-ahng bow) | 墙报 |
| **war** | *zhanzheng* (jahn-jerng) | 战争 |
| **watermelon** | *xigua* (she-gwah) | 西瓜 |
| **wealthy** | *youqian* (yoe-chee-an) | 有钱 |
| **wedding** | *hunli* (hwun-lee) | 婚礼 |

| weekend | *zhoumo* (joe-mwo) 周末 |
| welcome | *huanying* (hwahn-eeng) 欢迎 |
| west | *xi* (she) 西 |
| West (world) | *Xibian* (She-bee-an) 西边 |
| Western country | *Xiyang* (She-yahng) 西洋 |
| Western toilet | *Zuoshi cesuo* (Tswoh-shr tser-swoh) 作式厕所 |
| wildlife | *yeshengdongwu* (yeh-sherng-dohng-woo) 野生动物 |
| wind | *feng* (ferng) 风 |
| windy | *guafeng* (gwah-ferng) 刮风 |
| world | *shijie* (shr-jeh) 世界 |
| wristwatch | *hou biao* (show bee-ow) 手表 |
| writer | *zuojia* (zwoh-jah) 作家 |

## [X]

| xerox | *fuyin* (foo-een) 复印 |
| x-ray | *x-guangpianzi* (x-gwahng-pee-an-dzu) X- 光片子 |

## [Y]

| Yangtse River | *Chang Jiang* (Chahng Jee-ahng) 长江 |
| Yellow River | *Huang He* (Hwahng Her) 黄河 |
| yogurt | *suanrurao* (swahn-roo-rao) 酸乳酪 |
| young | *nianqing* (nee-an-cheeng) 年轻 |
| youth | *qingnian* (chee-ahng-nee-an) 青年 |

## [Z]

| zero | *ling* (leeng) 零 |
| zipper | *lalian* (lah-lee-an) 拉链 |
| zoo | *dongwuyuan* (dohng-woo-ywahn) 动物园 |